We Once Were a

THE DISSAPEARANCE OF BLACK CULTURE AND SOUL

STORY TOLD AND WRITTEN BY

FRANK ZAAQAN JORDAN

We Once Were a Family

STORY TOLD AND WRITTEN BY

FRANK ZAAQAN JORDAN

We Once Were a Family

The Disappearance of Black Culture and Soul

Story told and Written by, Frank Zaaqan Jordan

First Edition-Printing

Zaaqan1212@yahoo.com

ISBN #13- 9871088472736

We Once Were a Family

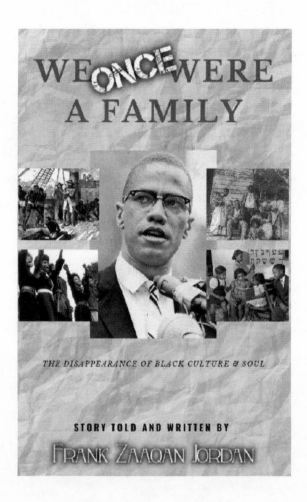

Story told and Written by, Frank Zaaqan Jordan

Introduction

Many may question in past recent decades how it is possible for an entire nation of individuals to have been captured together against their will brought to another land and stripped of their culture, integrity, and morals. During the Trans- Atlantic Slave Trade which lasted from the early 1500's into the late to early 1800's. This was a time period in which the French, Spanish, Arab, South Western Africans, along with the Europeans bought, and traded Black Hebrew engineers, mathematicians, leather shoe makers, craftsmen, physicians, mid-wives, master farmers, astrologists, blacksmiths, gold artificers, scribes, world-culture scholars, translators of multi languages, brick layers, inventors, Kings, and Queens during centuries of slave trading.

In the course of doing so, the entire American society was blueprinted, engineered, and brought fourth courteous of the Blacks that were hand selected, captured, and forced into the heinous conditions of slavery to bring together what now is known as the United States of America.

As far back as history was recorded Blacks, Native Americans, along with the Taino, and Boriqua Indians have always set a standard for family traditions and values. Once the American influences have saturated into our minds and spirit we then subconsciously from everyday habit forming practices, we then pass these ways of thinking and embracing a non-practical way of normalcy Europeans have embedded into our minds unto our children. We have always been a rich cultured society from black wealth, owning our very own societies with a banking system, farming communities, educational systems, medical care, hospitals, too financially recycling the black dollars within our self-reliant communities. Black culture isn't something that's purchased at a retail store, or found in a doctor's office through therapy sessions.

Black culture is inherited rightfully so through the spirit and seed of our great forefathers and ancestors, our great ability to adapt through unmentionable degrading and harsh circumstances along with unmeasurable odds throughout history, and still remain a trillion dollar asset to the world.

Black soul is more than just a name that you hear, Black culture is the beginning of mankind, and the beginning of creation. Black soul is what other nations have long desired to possess, Black soul is what many would die and kill to have except our own. Black culture is a gift from the heavenly Father above, Black soul is also what many nations have recognized as the force of power behind the entire universe.

Black culture and soul is the very component that's vanishing before our very eyes into the hands of our modern day oppressors for financial gain that's not reciprocated back into our communities.

Black soul and culture is the very essence of life.

Frank Zaaqan Jordan.

"For thou art an holy people unto the Lord thy God, the Lord hath chosen thee to be a special people (Israelites) unto himself, above all people that are upon the face of the earth"

Deuteronomy 7:6

"For the Lord hath chosen Jacob unto himself, and Israel for his peculiar treasure"

Psalms 135:4

" O ye seed of Israel his servant, ye children of Jacob, his chosen ones"

1Chronicles 16:13

"Truly *in vain is salvation hoped for from the hills, and from the multitude of mountains; truly in the Lord our God is salvation of Israel"*

Jeremiah 3:23

Contents

Chapter 1

What Happened?

Black pride in the 1920's - 1960's,

Many blacks today across the world may sit and ask themselves why does change happen, or even more so why does every generation seem to lack moral values, or the great integrity our fore fathers and mothers have once incorporated into our daily lives and routine. You ever ask yourself why the very quality of life seems to lack the basic fundamentals of class and functional everyday substances we need for survival.

Why are there less or a smaller percentage of black fathers in the home oppose to Caucasian homes whereas the percentage rate of single family homes in the Black community in 2007 was 65 percent , White communities had a single family home rate of 23 percent. In 2016 in the Black household the single parent rate rose to 66 percent, in the Caucasian household it barely rose to 24 percent. Despite this American economy was booming for the working class in the 50's as the US became the manufacturing king of the world following ww2. One of the reasons you see so many blacks within major cities or city limits today is due to their migration to the manufacturing cities such as Chicago, New York, New Jersey, and Detroit. Blacks migrated from the southern states in search of better and more consistent profitable jobs with benefits and work unions to offer as stability. By the time the 70's came around manufacturing started to dry up as American companies started looking towards cheaper labor and manufacturing opportunities overseas. The black family dynamics and culture was also very much intact in the 50's and most black children were born of two parent households unlike today where just the opposite is the case.

SEGREGATION

Noun; the action or state of setting someone or something apart from other people or things or being set apart; the enforced separation of different racial groups in a country, community, or establishment. [Ref; Meridian – Webster Dictionary]

The separation or isolation of race, class or ethnic group by enforced, or voluntary residence in a restricted area, by barriers to social intercourse, by separate educational facilities, or by discriminating means. [Ref; English Oxford Dictionary]

Black family structure in the 1950's was quite different, blacks all over the country lived in *SEGREGATION.* In the south, where over 70percent of blacks lived, that segregation was supported as whites there thought they would take over cause of high numbers in the region. Being not a full century from hard-core slavery Blacks in America in the 1950's were flourishing financially and culturally, these great-great-great grandchildren of the direct descend-ants from slaves were running hometown businesses in their communities, owned large amounts of land throughout the U.S, and they also developed, and controlled the wealth in their own Black-owned communities and neigh-borhoods. The black family dollar was recycled more within our own neigh-borhoods in the 1950's, unlike today with the ratio of the black dollar being re-cycled within a black community is at an all-time low of just 2 times daily, com-pared to the 1950's of a rate of being recycled at 35 times a day before it would reach another ethnicity of race other than blacks.

Once segregated away from other races of ethnicity, most black communities had very little option as to rely and depend on one another, as the result of be-ing segregated and isolated away from white Americans within the U.S. Our validation for being self-reliant was unquestionably the very best thing for us as an ethnic race of people.

Jim Crow Laws:

In the Plessy versus Ferguson case of 1896, the U.S Supreme Court ruled that the states had the legal power to require segregation between Blacks and Whites. Jim Crow laws spread across the south virtually anywhere the two races (Black and White) might or may come into contact. In the North and Mid-West, segregation was equally entrenched through informal customs and practices, many of these laws and practices lasted into the 1960's, until out-lawed by the 1964 Civil Rights Act.

Jim Crow

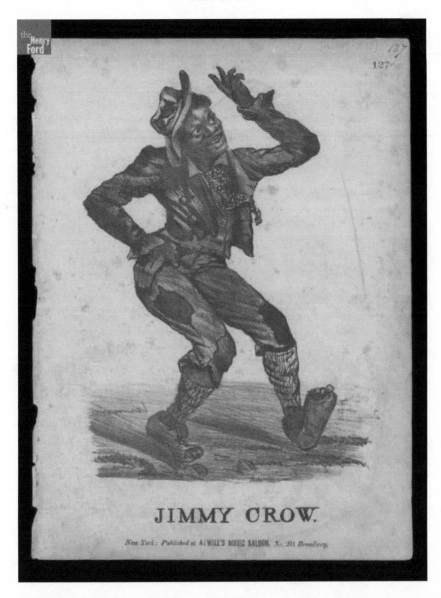

JIMMY CROW.

New York: Published at ATWILL'S MUSIC SALOON, No. 201 Broadway,

Jim Crow was a character first created for a minstrel-show act during the 1830's.the act featuring a white actor wearing black make-up, was meant to demean and make fun of Blacks. Applied to the later set of laws and practices, the name had much of the same effect.

Unmentioned Black wealth, neighborhoods and businesses during segregation.

The Hotel Theresa, Harlem NY

Hotel Theresa, located on Adam Clayton Powell Jr. Blvd, Harlem, NY

This 13-story hotel was built in 1912-13, by German born stock broker Gustavas Sidenberg (1843-1915), whose wife the hotel is named after, and was designed by the firm of George & Edward Blum, who specialized in designing apartment buildings. The hotel, which was known in its heyday as "The Waldorf of Harlem", exemplifies the Blums inventive use of terra-cotta for ornamentation, and has been called "one of the most visually striking structures in northern Manhattan."

The building, now an office building known as Theresa Towers, was designated a New York City landmark in 1993 and was added to the National Register of Historic Places in 2005.

Opened in 1913 and was, until the construction of the Adam Clayton Powell building across the street in 1973, the tallest building in Harlem. Primarily an apartment hotel, but also accepted temporary guest as well. It was bought by Love B. Woods, an African American businessman in 1937.

The hotel had a two-story penthouse dining room which featured views of Long Island Sound to the east and the Palisades to the west, as well as a bar and grill. In the 1940's and 1950's, the Theresa became a center of the social life of the black community of Harlem; the hotel profited from the refusal of prestigious hotels elsewhere in the city to accept black guest. As a result, black businessmen, performers, and athletes were thrown under the same roof. The building was also the location of such institutions as A. Philip's March on Washington Movement, the March Community Bookstore, and the Organization of Afro-American Unity created by Malcom X after he left the Nation of Islam.

The Hotel Theresa

Black owned Hotel Theresa, located on 125th street and Adam Clayton Powell, Harlem, N.Y.

Hotel Theresa

In 1960, Fidel Castro came to New York for the opening session of the United Nations, Castro and his entourage stayed at the Theresa, where they rented 80 rooms for $800 per day. Malcom X and other civil rights leaders arranged for their stay.

In October 1960, John Kennedy campaigned for the presidency at the hotel, along with Eleanor Roosevelt and other leading figures in the Democratic Party.

Notable guests, tenants, and employees at the Hotel Theresa.

- Muhammad Ali- boxer
- Louis Armstrong- musician, singer
- Josephine Baker- dancer
- Ron Brown- politician
- Fidel Castro- President of Cuba
- Ray Charles- singer, musician
- Kenneth Clark- educator
- Sam Cooke- singer, musician
- Dorothy Dandridge- actress
- Duke Ellington- jazz musician, composer, band leader
- Jimi Hendrix- rock musician
- Lena Horne- singer
- A. Philip Randolph- activist, anti-poverty leader
- Little Richard- singer, musician
- Joe Louis- boxer
- Sugar Ray Robinson- boxer
- Dinah Washington- singer

Notes [Aaron, Amanda. "Hotel Theresa" in Jackson, Kenneth T. ed 2010, Yale University Press, Wilson, Sondra Kathryn, Meet Me at the Theresa.]

The Green Book

Victor Hugo Green, was author, and brain-child of this great guide called "Negroe Motorist Green Book"

For nearly 30 years, a guide called the *"Negroe Motorist Green Book"* provided African Americans with advice on safe places to eat and sleep when they traveled through the Jim Crow- era United States. First published in 1936, this book was the brain-child of a Harlem based postal carrier named Victor Hugo Green. Like most Black Americans in the mid-20th century, Green had grown weary of the discrimination blacks faced whenever they ventured outside their neighborhoods. In the pages that , they provided a rundown of hotels, best housing, service stations, drug stores, taverns, barbershops and restaurants that were known to be owned and safe ports for black American travelers. The "Green Book" listed establishments in segregationist strongholds such as Alabama and Mississippi, but its reach also extended to Connecticut to California- any place where its readers might face prejudice or danger because of their skin color. With Jim Crow laws still looming over much of the country, a motto on the guides cover also doubled as a warning: "Carry your Green Book with you- You may need it."

Rates of car ownership had exploded in the years before and after World War II, but the lure of the interstate was also fought with risks for Blacks. "Whites Only" policies meant that black travelers often couldn't find safe places to eat and sleep, and so-called "Sundown Towns, municipalities that banned blacks after dark were scattered across the country. As the forwarded edition of the 1956 edition of the Green Book noted, "The White traveler has had no difficulty in getting accommodations, but with the negroe it has been different."

The Negroe Green Book 1936

The Green Book

While automobiles made it much easier for black Americans to be inde-
pendently mobile, the difficulties they faced in traveling were such that, as
Lester B. Granger of the national Urban League puts it, "so far as travel is
concerned, Negroes are America's last pioneers." Black travelers often had
to carry buckets or portable toilets in the trunks of their cars because they
were usually barred from bathrooms and rest areas in service stations and
roadside stops. Travel essentials such as gasoline were difficult to purchase
because of discrimination at gas stations.

To avoid such problems on long trips, Blacks often packed meals and carried
containers of gasoline in their cars. Writing of the road trips that he made as a
young child in the 1950's Courtland Milloy of the *Washington Post* recalled
that his mother spent the evening before the trip frying chicken and boiling
eggs so that his family would have something to eat along the way the next
day.

Blacks often had to spend hours in the evening trying to find somewhere to
stay, sometimes resorting to sleeping in haylofts or in their own cars if they
could not find anywhere. One alternative, if it was available, was to arrange in
advance to sleep at the homes of black friends in towns or cities along their
route.

The civil rights leader John Lewis has recalled how his family prepared for a
trip in 1951:

"There would be no restaurant for us to stop at until we were out of the south,
so we took our restaurant right in the car with us......Stopping for gas and to
use the bathroom took careful planning. Uncle Otis had made this trip before,
and he knew the places along the way offered "colored" bathrooms and which
were better just to pass on by. Our map was marked and our route was
planned that way, by the distances between service stations where it would
be safe for us to stop."

Finding accommodations was one of the greatest challenges faced by black
travelers. The Green Book's principle goal was to provide accurate information on Black friendly accommodations to answer the constant question
that faced black drivers: "Where will you spend the night?" As well as essen-
tial information on lodges, service stations, and garages, it provided details of
leisure facilities open to black Americans including beauty salons, restaurants, night clubs and country clubs. The listings focused on four main cate-
gories- hotels, motels, tourist homes (private residences, usually owned by
blacks, which provided accommodations to black travelers), and restaurants.

They were arranged by state and subdivided by city, giving the name and address of each business.

The Gilmore Museum located In Hickory Corners, MI showcases the near-forgotten Guide Book for African American travelers.

Notes: [The Negroe Motorist Green Book; Wikipedia]

Black Bottom, Detroit, MI

Located northeast of downtown, Black Bottom was bound by Gratiot, Brush, Vernor and the Grand Trunk railroad. In the 1900's, many blacks migrated north of Detroit seeking employment in the cities growing industries. Racially discriminative housing covenants forced most of them to settle in Black Bottom, altering the connotation of the district. As thousands of blacks streamed into Black Bottom, the community swelled with vibrant cultural, educational and social amenities.

The site of Lafayette Park has a long, controversial history that precedes the modernist urban development. Centuries before Lafayette Park was built, French settlers farmed the area and named it "Black Bottom" for its dark, fertile soil and elevation. In the twentieth century, Black Bottom became one of the most vibrant black American districts in Detroit.

The district reached its social, culture and political peak in 1920.Blacks owned 350 businesses in Detroit, most within Black Bottom. The community additionally boasted 17 physicians, 22 lawyers, 22 barbershops, 13 dental offices, 12 tailors, 10 restaurants, 10 real estate dealers, 8 grocers, 6 drugstores, 5 undertakers, 4 employment agencies.

Towards the end of the decade, black employment in Detroit dropped almost 30%.the stock market crashed only exacerbated the dire circumstances of Black Bottom's working class families.

1930's. following the stock market crash in 1929, the United States entered into the Great Depression. Soaring unemployment of the 1930's remains unparalleled in American History. President Franklin D. Roosevelt attempted to ameliorate the high unemployment rate, and extreme housing conditions of many working class Americans through his New Deal initiatives for thousands of Blacks living in Black Bottom, this meant the construction of the nation's first black public housing development, the Brewster housing projects.

The Brewster projects covered 15 city blocks and were comprised of two-and three story townhomes. First lady Eleanor Roosevelt was present at the groundbreaking, which was a celebrity event for the Black Bottom community. By 1938 more units were available to tenants, and 240 additional units were constructed over the next three years. At its peak Brewster Homes were home to 8,000-10,000 residents, including future Motown artists Stevie Wonder and Diana Ross. Joe Louis began his boxing career at the Brewster recreation Center. In 1951,140,000 blacks resided and rented in Black Bottom.

Black Bottom, Detroit MI, 1930's

Fig.1 *1801 ‑ 03. MONROE.*

Blacks flourished during 1930's in their own communities

Fig.2

Barthwell's Drugs, and Pharmacy Black Bottom Detroit, MI 1930's

Black Bottom, Detroit MI 1930's

Hastings Street, Detroit, MI, Black owned community

Black owner of Sidney Barthwell and Barthwell's Pharmacy one of six, located in Black Bottom Detroit, MI

Paradise Valley, Detroit MI

Paradise Valley was the adjoining neighborhood to the north, where bars and clubs filled the main thoroughfare- Hastings Street. Music and danced spilled into the streets. Jazz, Blues, and the early notes of rock and soul. Hastings and St. Antoine led north to Paradise Valley, often called Detroit's Las Vegas for its extravagant nightlife.

Although Black bottom are often remembered as one large cultural hub, they were two separate areas on Hastings Street. Paradise Valley is believed to have been located downtown where I-75, Comerica Park and Ford field now stand, but its exact boundaries are often debated. The last traces of the Valley disappeared when its three remaining buildings were finally razed in 200. Only few clues would indicate that it even existed, most notably the single Michigan Historical Site marker on the former intersection of Adams Avenue and St. Antoine Street.

Paradise Theatre

- *The Paradise Theatre located in Detroit, MI, housed several clusters of early jazz clubs in the 1920's. By the 1930's, roughly two dozen jazz clubs filled the area. Places such as 606 Horseshoe Lounge and Club Three Sixes featured national acts including Duke*

- *Ellington, Diana Washington, and Sarah Vaughan, plus other greats such as Billie Holiday, Ella Fitzgerald, Dizzy Gillespie, Billy Eckstine, and Count Basie.*

The Greystone Ball Room

The Greystone Ballroom was a Dancehall located in Detroit, MI opened in 1922 to hold 3,000 people, Was known as the largest Ballroom at that time in the city.

The Greystone Ballroom, meanwhile, was the cities cradle of jazz, opened in 1922,it was once Detroit's largest and grandest ballroom.in 1974 interview with the Detroit News, clarinetist Benny Goodman said he drove all night to catch Bix Beiderbecke at the Greystone, calling it " a great mecca in those days". During the height of big band jazz, the Greystone often hosted a battle of bands, with one in particular between Ellington and McKinney's Cotton Pickers that drew a record breaking crowd of around 7,000.

In 1942, The Detroit Urban League reported that within Black Bottom and Paradise Valley were:

- 151 Physicians
- 140 Social Workers
- 85 Lawyers
- 71 Beauty Shops
- 57 Restaurants
- 36 Dentists
- 30 Drug Stores
- 25 Barber Shops
- 25 Dress Maker Shops
- 20 Hotels
- 15 Fish and poultry markets
- 10 Hospitals
- 10 Electricians
- 9 insurance Companies
- 7 Building Contractors
- 5 Flower Shops
- 2 Bondsmen
- 2 Dairy Distributors

"Negroes had it made in Detroit until World War II," said Sidney Barthwell, who owned several drugstores throughout the Black Bottom and Paradise Valley. "We had about everything we needed in the Black business community. Discrimination gave us tremendous (economic) power because we had been compacted in a small area"

[Notes; Black Bottom and Paradise Valley: Center of black life in Detroit, Michigan Chronicle]

The Provident Hospital, Chicago

Dr.Daniel Hale Williams

Provident Hospital

In 1889, Emma Reynolds, a young women who aspired to be a nurse, was denied admission by each of Chicago's nursing schools on the grounds that she was black. Her brother, the reverend Louis Reynolds, pastor of St. Stephens African Methodist Episcopal Church, approached the respected black surgeon, Dr.Daniel Hale Williams for help. Unable to influence the existing schools, they decided to launch a new nursing school for black women.in 1890, Dr.Williams consulted with a group of black ministers, physicians, and businessmen to explore establishing a nurse-training facility and hospital.

There were only a few black physicians in Chicago at this time, and all had limited to no hospital privileges. The community leaders assured him of their support and the energetic fund-raising began.

Rallies were scheduled on Chicago's south and west sides. The donations included supplies, equipment, and financial support.one of the most important early contributions came in 1890 when Clergyman Reverend Jenkins Jones secured a commitment from the Armour Meat Packing Company for the down payment on a three-story brick hose at 29th and Dearborn. This building, with 12 beds, became the first Provident Hospital.

Provident Hospital

Provident Hospital, Chicago, Ill, 1891

Although the hospitals formation was dependent on wealthy donors, and affluent donors stepped in at key moments in Providents history, the generosity of community residents was also a critical factor.

Community support was not restricted to financial contributions. The strong appeal of a hospital responsive to the black community elicited repeated waves of community volunteerism. Black residents, workers, public officials, church leaders contributed heavily to opening and sustaining the facility.

The legal papers were drawn up in 1891 for "Provident Hospital and Training School Association" and the charter school stated: "The object for which it is formed is to maintain a hospital and training school for nurses in the City of Chicago, Illinois, for the gratuitous treatment of the medical and surgical disease of the sick poor"

As demand for medical care grew, the Provident board initiated planning to expand. An 1896 funding campaign raised sufficient funding to construct a new building on donated land at 36th and Dearborn. The effort was helped by abolitionist Fredrick Douglass, who gave a public lecture in Chicago and presented a donation at the hospital site to Dr. Williams. By 1897, the hospital had 189 inpatients, and the outpatient clinic, the Armour Dispensary, treated, treated approximately 6,000 patients. In 1898, the hospital moved to the new 36th street location, which had 65 beds.

All Black doctor and nursing staff at the Provident Hospital 1891

- *Dr. Daniel Hale Williams born January 18th, 1856, in Hollidaysburg, Penn. Daniel Hale Williams pursued a pioneering career in medicine, in 1893 Williams opened Provident Hospital.*
- *He also was the first black physicians to successfully perform and complete pericardial (open-heart) surgery on a patient.*

[Notes; Hektoen International, a journal of Medical Humanities]

The Wheatley-Provident Hospital, Chicago, Ill

<u>*Provident Hospital was the very first Black owned and operated medical institution in the United States*</u>

Provident Hospital, 1856 Chicago Illinois

Annie Minerva Turnbo Malone (August 9, 1869- May 10, 1957) was a Black businesswomen, educator, inventor and philanthropist. Annie also was two years younger than Madam C.J Walker. She had launched her hair care business four years before Sarah Breedlove (later known as C.J Walker).in the early 1900's Madam C.J Walker worked as a "Poro Agent" for Annie for about a year.

In the first three decades of the 20th century, she founded and developed a large and prominent commercial and educational enterprise centered around cosmetics for and specifically for Black women. Annie was born in Metropolis to former slaves. She was the tenth of eleven children born to Robert Turnbo, a poor farmer, and Isabella Cook Turnbo. Because her parents died when she was young. Annie was raised by her older sister in nearby Peoria, Illinois. She was a sickly child and missed a lot of school which resulted in her having to withdraw before completing high school.

By the beginning of 1900's Annie Malone began to revolutionize hair care methods for all blacks. Armed with this revolutionary formula and a product she called "The Great Wonderful Hair Grower" Annie moved to St. Louis in 1902. She hired some assistants and began selling her products door-to-door.

Malone called it *Poro, a West African (Mende) male secret or devotional society.*

Poro College

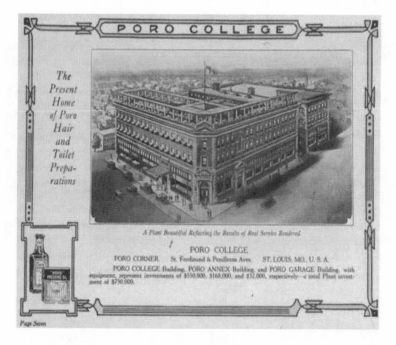

The
Present
Home
of Poro
Hair
and
Toilet
Prepa-
rations

PORO COLLEGE

A Plant Beautiful Reflecting the Results of Real Service Rendered

PORO COLLEGE

PORO CORNER   St. Ferdinand & Pendleton Aves.   ST. LOUIS, MO., U. S. A.

PORO COLLEGE Building, PORO ANNEX Building, and PORO GARAGE Building, with equipment, represent investments of $550,000, $168,000, and $32,000, respectively—a total Plant investment of $750,000.

Page Seven

Poro College founded by Annie Malone, 1917

By 1917, as the United States entered World War I, Annie Malone had become so successful that she founded and opened Poro College in St. Louis. It was the first educational institution in the United States dedicated to the study and teaching of black cosmetology. The school reportedly graduated over 75,000 agents world-wide, including the Caribbean. The school employed nearly 200 blacks. Its curriculum included instructions to train students on personal style to present themselves at work, walking, talking, talking and style of dress designed to maintain a solid public persona. The Poro College building was later purchased by St. James African-Methodist Episcopal (AME) Church and demolished in 1965 to construct The James House.

Malone donated large sums to countless charities. During the 1920's, Malone's philanthropy included financing the education of two full time students in every historically black college in the country.

The Poro College Diploma awarded upon completion of the course

Vintage photo of Poro graduation class, founder Annie Malone pictured in the back row, with glasses.

Madam C.J Walker

Sarah Breedlove, later known as Madam C.J Walker

Sarah Breedlove- who later would come to be known as Madam C.J. Walker-
was born on December 23, 1867 on the same Delta, Louisiana plantation
where her parents, Owen and Minerva Anderson Breedlove, had been enslaved before the end of the Civil War. This child of sharecroppers trans-
formed herself from an uneducated farm laborer and laundress into one of the
twentieth century's most successful, self-made women entrepreneurs.

During the 1890's, Sarah began to suffer from a scalp ailment that caused her
to lose most of her hair. She consulted her brothers for advice and also exper-
imented with many homemade remedies and store- bought products, including those made by Annie Malone. In 1905 Sarah moved to. Denver as a sales
agent for Annie Malone, then married her third husband, Charles Joseph
Walker, a St. Louis newspaperman. After changing her name to "Madam" C.J
Walker, she founded her own business and began selling Madam Walker's
Wonderful hair Grower, a scalp conditioning and healing formula, which she
claimed had to been revealed to her in a dream. Madam Walker, by the way,
did NOT invent the straightening comb or chemical perms, though many people incorrectly believe that to be true.

By early 1910, she had settled in Indianapolis, then the nation's largest inland
manufacturing center, where she built a factory, hair and manicure salon and

another training school. Less than a year after her arrival, Walker grabbed national headlines in the black press when she contributed $1,000 to the building fund of the "colored" YMCA in Indianapolis.

Walker herself moved to New York in 1916, leaving the day-to day operations of the Madam C.J Walker Manufacturing Company in Indianapolis to Ransom and Alice Kelly, her factory forelady and a former school teacher. She continued to oversee the business and to work in the New York office. Once in Harlem, she quickly became involved in Harlem's social and political life, taking special interest in the NAACP's anti-lynching movement to which she contributed $5,000.

As her business continued to grow, Walker organized her agents into local and state clubs. Her Madam C.J Walker Hair Culturists Union of America convention in Philadelphia in 1917 must have been one of the first national meetings of business women in the country. Walker used the gathering not only to reward her agents for their business success, but to encourage their political activism as well. "This is the greatest country under the sun," she told them."

By the time she died at her estate, Villa Lewaro, in Irvington-on-Hudson, New York, she had helped create the role of the 20th Century, self-made American Businesswomen :established herself as a pioneer of the modern black-hair-care and cosmetics industry; and set standards in the African American community for corporate and community giving.

[*Notes; Madam C.J Walker: A Brief Biographical Essay, by A'Lelia Bundles*]

Annie Malone and Madam C.J Walker Products

Wonderful Hair Grower

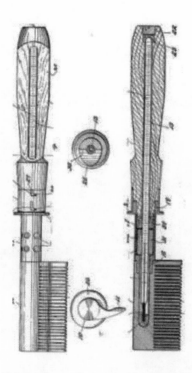

The Hot Comb was first patent by Annie Malone

A.G. Gaston

A.G Gaston (right) standing in front of his motel located in Birmingham, AL

The Gaston Motel, built and constructed in 1954 by black businessman A.G Gaston.

A.G Gaston Motel

The Gaston Motel is a former motel located at 1510 5ᵗʰ avenue north, now part of Birmingham's "Civil Rights District". It was constructed in 1954 by businessman A.G Gaston to provide higher-class service to black visitors during the cities decades of strictly segregated businesses and recreation.

Gaston struck upon the idea of building a motel while he and his wife visited Europe for an international Methodist conference in the summer of 1951. He had heard that the National Baptist Convention's Sunday School and Baptist Training Union Congress was considering Birmingham for its 1954 meeting. Knowing that black visitors would have trouble finding adequate lodging, he set out to fill the need. After his return he studied motels, especially the Holiday Inn chain, which served as a model for the Gaston Motel.

The Gaston Motel opened on June 30, 1954, just in time to host guests of the National Baptist Convention. The Motel had 32 guest rooms, some of which were "master suites" which could sleep up to seven guests. All rooms were heated and air-conditioned with private baths, in-room telephones, and jukeboxes. The drapes and bedspreads were custom made and high end furniture were purchased from Rhodes Carroll.

The lounge regularly booked nationally-renowned entertainers, *including Little Richard and Stevie Wonder. Notable guests included Duke Ellington, Count Basie, Harry Belafonte, Johnny Mathis, Nat King Cole, Aretha Franklin, and Jackie Robinson. Future Secretary of State Colin Powell* spent his wedding night there with his bride Alma on August 25, 1962.

Outlining plans for expansion, Gaston checks blueprint. Million-dollar Gaston Building (right) is heart of vast Gaston empire. Housed in building are Gaston-owned or controlled Citizens Federal Savings and Loan Association, Booker T. Washington Insurance Company, Booker T. Washington Business College and an investment company.

The Unveiled plans for the expansion of the Gaston Motel in 1977

[References Sutton, Marie, (2014 The A.G Gaston Motel in Birmingham]

Old Walnut Street, Louisville KY

If you are a Louisville local, you may have heard of the old Walnut Street business district (now Muhammad Ali Boulevard). West Walnut Street from 6th to 13th streets was a business, social, and cultural gathering place for African Americans. Beginning in the late 1800's, the first black business started to form on and around Walnut Street, and it grew to include over 150 black owned businesses. The area serve a vital need during segregation, and thrived especially from the 1920's to the 1950's.

Although this area was demolished during urban renewal, it holds a special place in the hearts and the memories of many African Americans in the Louisville community. By the 1900's the number of black owned businesses grew to 24, and that number grew to over 150 by the 1930's. The growth continued through the 40's, but began to decline in the 1950's.

Stated reasons for the decline and ultimate closing of the business district include: desegregation (many black residents took opportunities to shop in areas that were previously prohibited), the migration of many white residents to the suburbs, and finally urban renewal which later wiped out most of the businesses and resident homes in 1960's.

The businesses that dotted old Walnut Street included those for everyday needs like restaurants, churches, banks, insurance companies, news and printing services, barber shops, salons, gas stations, independent doctors, lawyers, real estate agents, and more. However, the area was well known for the entertainment including several theaters, night clubs, and gathering places. Clubs like Top Hat drew crowds from out of town, as well as local residents who came to see the top musicians of the time. Derby was popular time on Walnut Street.

Theaters such as the lyric, the Grand, and the Lincoln were also noted as popular entertainment spots. Other businesses included Mammoth Life and Accident Insurance, First Standard Bank.

[*References, encyclopedia of Louisville, African American Businesses*]

First Standard Bank, Black Owned during Segregation 1920's, Old Walnut street, Louisville, KY

Black business neighborhood, Old Walnut street Louisville, KY

Mammoth Life and Accident Insurance

Black Businesses men Henry E. Hall a Kentucky native and William H. Wright, a lawyer from Alabama, were the founders of Mammoth Life and Accident Insurance Company, located at 422 S. 6th street in Louisville, constructed in 1926.

[Ref; Notable Kentucky Americans Database]

The Ohio Theater

The Art deco style Ohio Theatre opened during 1941. Seating was listed at 900.

[Ref; Cinema Treasures]

Hayti District of Durham, N.C

In the early twentieth century, Parrish Street in Durham what constituted what today would be called an enterprise zone, propelled by the Bull City's Black businessmen. Nationally recognized, the business district acquired the nickname "Black Wall Street." The four- block area completed the Hayti community just to the south, the principal residential district for black Durham residents and center of the city's educational, cultural, and religious life. In a period when race relations elsewhere in North Carolina were at an all-time low,Durhams black businessmen, with the tacit support(or tolerance, at any rate)of their white counterparts, made strides.

John Merrick(/biography/merrick-john), Dr.Aaron Moore(/biography/moore-aaron-mcduffie),and C.C. Spaulding(/biography/Spaulding-charles-clinton-O), the "Triumvirate" at the head of North Carolina Mutual Life Insurance Company, the nation's largest black-owned insurance company, moved their headquarters in 1906 to Parrish, to be joined by Mechanics and Farmers Bank, founded by R.B. Fitzgerald and W.G. Person, in 1907.the Mutual leaders had other ventures, among them real estate and textiles. When W.E.B. Du Bois visited in 1912, he recorded an unparalleled level of black entrepreneurship, crediting the tolerate attitude of the city's whites and writing "it's is precisely the opposite spirit in places like Atlanta."

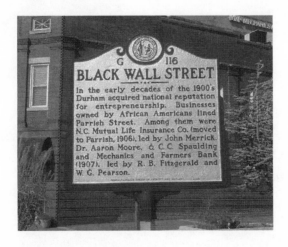

Black Wall Street is a term that describes historic Parrish Street, a four block area downtown Durham, where Black enterprise thrived in the late 1800s and early 1900s. The term came into use in the 1950s and references the famous financial district in New York City. During the early 1900s, similar black business districts had developed in other cities, but Durham earned a national reputation. In response to reconstruction in the late 1800's, southern states passed Jim Crow laws to enforce segregation and limit opportunities of Blacks.

[Reference"Durhams Black Wall Street, NC School of Education, UNC University]

North Carolina Mutual Life Insurance Company

Figure 1.* Founder and owner of the North Carolina Mutual Insurance Life Insurance Company John Merrick (1859-1919), was a black entrepreneur whose life represents a rags-to-riches story. Born into slavery in Clinton, North Carolina Merrick relied on his social savvy, and inner drive to achieve and amass great personal wealth by founding various companies in Raleigh, North Carolina, and Durham, North Carolina areas. Portions of his wealth were channeled and recycled back into the black community through philanthropy.

Figure 2. * The North Carolina Mutual life Insurance Company, formed in 1898 by black businessman John Merrick.

[*Reference, McCants Andrews, John Merrick; A biographical Sketch (Durham Press, 1920]*

Durham (cont.);

The North Carolina Mutual Life Company

Black businessman John Merrick founded the North Carolina Mutual Life Insurance Company, located in Durham, NC

Ariel night view of NC Mutual Life Insurance Company

Biltmore Hotel, Grill, Restaurant

The Biltmore Hotel, Durham N.C 330-332 East Pettigrew Street, Built 1929

The Biltmore Hotel was built in 1923 by Dr.Clyde Donnell, built min the pre-eminent area of Hayti in the segregated era, one of the pre-eminent hotels that strictly catered to Blacks in the southeast. Artist, educators, and just visitors came to see the "big name bands "and would stay at this 30 room hotel when they came to town. The Biltmore featured also a drugstore and grill/coffee shop on the ground floor, the only one of its kind in the South at the time that exclusively catered to Negro patrons only.

Durham, NC (cont.);

Lincoln Hospital, Durham NC

1301 Fayetteville Street, Durham NC Built 1924

LINCOLN HOSPITAL NURSE TRAINING SCHOOL

The second incarnation of Lincoln Hospital was located at 1301 Fayetteville St, replacing the earlier structure at the northwest corner of Proctor St. and Cozart St. The Hospital had been established at that earlier site primarily through the advocacy of Dr. Aaron Moore. Dr.Moore strongly that the

Durham, NC (cont);

Black community should have their own hospital where Black physicians and nurses could practice. This institution also included a school of nursing, established in 1905 and provided internship/residency training for physicians.

(Courtesy Durham County Library/North Carolina Collection)

Well Baby Clinic, Durham, NC

Angier B.Duke Nurses Home

Angier B.Duke Nursing Home, 1946 (courtesy Durham County Library/North Carolina Collection)

Lincoln Hospital, Durham NC

Behind the main hospital building was a Nurses home, Ben Duke contributed $35,000 towards the Nurses Home; this was combined with funds from Dr. Moore's estate to furnish the rooms and provide equipment for classrooms. Dr. Charles Shepard proposed that nurses home to be named after Angier B.Duke, Ben Duke's son, who died in 1923.

Mechanics and farmers bank

"Portrait of some of the original black Founders of Mechanics & Farmers Bank, Durham, NC. (From the Durham County Library, via Learn NC.)

North Carolinas oldest Black- owned bank, was established in 1908 in Durham, NC, under the auspices of the North Carolina Mutual and Provident Association (re-named the North Carolina Mutual Life Insurance Company 1919). The original all black charter members included Richard Fitzgerald, John Merrick, Aaron Moore, William G. Pearson, J.C. Scarborough, Charles C. Spaulding, J.A. Dodson, and Stanford L. Warren.

The bank first operated from space in the building of the North Carolina Mutual and Provident Association, later moving to a building on West Parrish Street. Mechanics and Farmers became an important source of financing in the 1920s, saving more than 500 Black people farms and residences, when its loan department provided $200,000 in individual loans. The banks policy stated its intent to provide "no large loans".... To a few profiteers, but rather conservative sums to needy farmers and laborers. "The bank was one of about a dozen Black owned banks to survive the Great Depression, and holds the distinction of being the first lending institution in North Carolina to receive a Certificate of Authority from the Federal Housing Administration in 1935.

Durham, NC (cont.);

Mechanics and farmers bank

Mechanics and Farmers Bank established in 1908

Mechanics and Farmers Bank, Durham, NC

Chapter 2

Trusting Our Enemy

Integration the Decline Of The Black Community

Integration; the action or process of integrating; combination, amalgamation, incorporation, unification, consolidation, merger, blending.

Many individuals assume through emotional thoughts of opinions, coupled with tradition added with the absurd way society has taught us to join or to merge together as one nation, race or races to combine in the same space of living is perhaps the best way to co-habitat with one another. Assuming that was true, let's look at a historical time-line and chain of events which happened to blacks as a result of integrating with the representation of Europeans or government through-out our history.

"Indian Massacre" is a phrase whose use and definition has evolved and expanded over time. The phrase was initially used by European colonists to describe attacks by indigenous Americans which resulted in mass colonial casualties. While similar attacks on colonists on Indian villages were called "raids" or "battles", successful Indian attacks on white stolen settlements or military posts were routinely termed "massacres".

In *An American Genocide, The United States and the California Catastrophe, 1846-1873*, historian Benjamin Madley recorded the numbers of killings of California Indians alone between 1846 and 1873. He found evidence that during this period at least 9,400 to 16,000 California Indians were murdered by Europeans. Most of these killings occurred in what he said were more than 370 massacres (defined to him as the "intentional killing of five or more disarmed combatants or largely unarmed noncombatants, including women, children, and prisoners").

On these following pages is a list of some of the events reported then or referred to now as "Indian Massacre". This list contains only some recorded incidents that occurred in Canada or the United States, or territory presently part of the United States. Key words *"some of the recorded massacres"*, not all, the numbers in such cases are higher.

<u>Pre- Columbian era</u>

<u>Year- 1325, Crow Creek massacre, South Dakota-</u>

- 486 known dead were discovered at an archaeological site near Chamberlain, South Dakota. The victims and perpetrators were both unknown groups of Native Americans. <u>486 dead.</u>

<u>Columbian era and beyond, 1500-1830;</u>

<u>Year 1539, Napituca Massacre, Florida-</u>

- After defeating resisting Timucuan warriors, Hernando de Soto had 200 executed, in the first large-scale massacre by Europeans on what later became U.S. soil. <u>200 dead.</u>

<u>Year – 1601, Sandia Mountains, New Mexico-</u>

- Spanish troops destroyed 3 Indian villages in the Sandia Mountains, New Mexico. According to Spanish sources, over 900 Tompiro Indians were killed. <u>900 plus killed.</u>

<u>Year- 1623, May 12th, Pamunkey Peace Talks, Virginia-</u>

- The English poisoned the wine at a "peace conference" with Powhatan leaders, killing about 200; and physically attacked and killed another 50<u>. Killed 250</u>.

<u>Year- 1637, May 26th, Mystic Massacre, Connecticut-</u>

- English colonist commanded by John Mason, launched a night attack on a large Pequot Indian village on the Mystic River in present-day Connecticut, where they burned the inhabitants in their homes and killed all survivors, for total fatalities of about 600-700<u>. Murdered 600-700</u>.

<u>Year- 1644, March, Pound Ridge Massacre, New York-</u>

- As part of Keifts War in New Netherland, at this present day Pound Ridge, New York, John Underhill, hired by the Dutch, attacked and burned a sleeping Indian village of Lenape, killing about 500 unarmed Indians, women and children<u>. Murdered 500</u>.

Year- 1644 Massapequa Massacre, New York-

- John Underhill's men killed more than 100 Indians near present day Massa-pequa. <u>Killed 100</u>.

Year- 1712 May, Fox Indian Massacre, Michigan-

- French troops with killed around 1,000 Fox Indians men, women, and children in a five-day massacre near the head of the Detroit River<u>. Killed 1000.</u>

Year- 1730 September 9th, Massacre at Fox Fort, Quebec-

- A French army of 1,400 soldiers massacred about 500 Fox Indians (including 300 women and children) as they tried to flee their besieged camp. <u>Murdered 500.</u>

Year- 1747 October, Chama River, New Mexico-

- Spanish troops ambushed a group of Utes on the Chama River, killing 111 Indi-ans and taking 206 captives. <u>111 killed</u>.

Year 1774, Spanish Peaks, New Mexico-

- Spanish troops surprised a large fortified Comanche village near Spanish Peaks (Raton, New Mexico). They killed nearly 300 Indians (men, women, and children) and took 100 captives. <u>300 killed</u>.

<u>Pictured above is the Battle of Wounded Knee, South Dakota 1890, U.S 7th Calvary under James W. Forsyth massacred over 350 unarmed Indians men, women and children</u>.

(Integration) cont.

<u>Year 1805, January Canyon del Muerto, Arizona</u>-

- Spanish soldiers led by Antonio Narbona massacred 115 Navajo Indians (mostly women, children and old men), in Canyon del Muerto, north eastern Arizona<u>. Massacred 115</u>.

<u>Year 1833, Cutthoat Gap Massacre, Oklahoma</u>-

- The Osage tribe attacked a Kiowa camp west of the Wichita Mountains in southwest Oklahoma, killing 150 Kiowa Indians<u>. Killed 150</u>.

<u>Year 1846, April 6th, Sacramento River Massacre, California</u>-

- Captain Frémont's men attacked a band of Indians (probably Wintun) on the Sacramento River in California, killing between 120 and 200 Indians<u>. Killed 120-200</u>

British Patriot soldiers 1818 invading, and waging war on Indian Territory, enslaving women and children, and hanging the men on trees (background).

[References, Genocide an American Indian History, Jeffery Ostler; University of Oregon 2015]

[References, Steele, Ian Kenneth, Warpaths Invasion of North America, Oxford University Press]

Cherokee Indians

European settlers, along with Spanish conquers killed and murdered unarmed black Indian men, women and children by the hundreds during the invasion of their land.

Year 1851, Old Shasta Town, California-

- Miners killed 300 Wintu Indians near Old Shasta, California and burned down their tribal council meeting house. <u>Killed 300.</u>

Year 1864, Oak Run Massacre, California-

- California white settlers massacred 300 plus Yana Indians who had gathered near the head of Oak Run, California for a spiritual ceremony. <u>Massacred 300plus.</u>

Year 1864, November 29th, Sand Creek Massacre, Colorado-

- White members of the Colorado Militia attacked a peaceful black Indian village of Cheyenne, killing up to 163 men women and children at Sand Creek in Kiowa County. <u>Killed 70-163.</u>

[*References, American Holocaust: The Conquest of The New World, David E. Stannard, Oxford University Press, 1993 pg. 130*]

The Indian Removal Act of 1830

Indian Removal Act of 1830

The Indian Removal Act of 1830 gave US troops federal authority to banish Native American Indians from their homelands once and for all, including the Ohio Shawnee aborigines.

In Ohio, Shawnee lands and their personal possessions were then "legally" seized by the government and sold at public auction for pennies on the dollar....

- The Indian Removal Act was signed into law by President Andrew Jackson on May 28th 1830, authorizing the president to grant unsettled lands west of the Mississippi in exchange for Indian lands within existing state boarders. A few tribes went peacefully, but many resisted the relocation policy.
- Gold was discovered on Cherokee land.
- During the fall and winter of 1838 and 1839, the Cherokees were forcibly moved west by the United States government.
- Approximately 4,000 Cherokees died of bad weather exposure, and untreated diseases on this forced march of removal, which became known as the "Trail of Tears."
- President Jackson signed a law and ordered the Choctaws, Creek, Seminoles, Chickasaws, Cherokees, and other native tribes to leave their land.
- 100,000 plus native Indians were forcibly removed from their land, men, women, and children between 1830-1838.

[Reference, Library of Congress Legal]

Indian Removal Act 1830

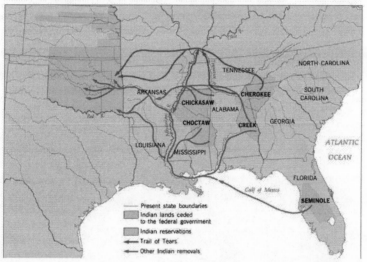

President Jackson (below) ordered the removal of natives from off their land by force by signing the Indian Removal Act in 1830

7th U.S President.

U.S. President Andrew Jackson in office from 1829-1837

(Integration) cont.;

Natives were forced off their land by European Settlers

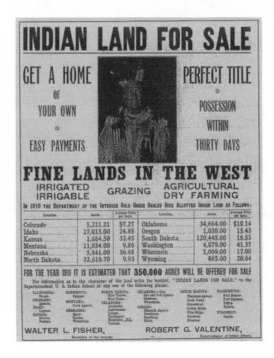

Spaniard Explorers

Fray Bartolome de las casas wrote about conquistadors training dogs to attack and kill natives.

Meaning of Conquistador*; one of Spanish conquerors of Indian tribes, and Mexico 16th century; literally "conqueror"*

"The Spaniards train their fierce dogs to attack, kill and tear to pieces the Indians...The Spaniards keep alive their dog's appetite for human beings in this way. They have Indians brought to them in chains, then unleash the dogs. The Indians come meekly down the roads and are killed. And the Spaniards have butcher shops where the corpse of Indians are hung up, on display, and someone will come in and say, more or less," Give me a quarter of that rascal hanging there, to feed my dogs until I can kill another one for them."

(Devastation of the Indies, by Fray Bartolome deLas Casas)

Spanish Conquistadors

Fay Bartolome de las Casas wrote about the brutality of The Spanish Conquistadors.

"They snatcht young babies from their mothers breasts, and then dash out their brains of those innocents against the rocks; others they cast into Rivers scoffing and jeering them, and call'd upon their bodies when falling with derision, the true testimony of their cruelty, to come to them, and inhumanely exposing others to their merciless Swords, together with the mothers that gave them life."

[The Devastation of the Indies, written by Fray Bartolome de las Casas]

(Integration) cont.;

Intentional Atrocities against the Native Indians

1451-1506

Spanish Conqueror Christopher Columbus is responsible for many onslaughts of massacres, and enslaving thousands of native Indians.

Numerous atrocities against Native American Indians span the hundreds of years from the first arrival of European explores to the modern era under a wide range of circumstances. Today there are over 500 Native American tribes in the United States, each with a distinct culture, way of life and history. Even today, Native Indians face extreme and large challenges today to cope with the disadvantages history has left them and ongoing cases of discrimination.

- 10 million plus estimated of Native Indians were living in the land that is now the United States when European explorers first arrived in the 15th century.
- Less than 300,000 estimated number of Native Indians were living in the United States around 1900.

By the time Christopher Columbus reached the Caribbean in 1942, historians' estimate there were 10 million indigenous peoples living in U.S. territory. But by 1900, that number had reduced to less than 300,000.

Disease was a major killer, followed by malnutrition. Colonists in search of gold staged violent, and murderous ambushes on Indian tribe villages, fueling animosity with Natives.

Disease

The most significant reason for the Native Indian decline was disease- an invisible killer that wiped out an estimated 90% of the population. Unlike Europeans and Asians, whose lifestyle had a long history of sharing close quarters with domesticated and wild animals, Native Indians were not immune to pathogens spread by domesticated cows, pigs, sheep, goats, and horses. As a result, millions were killed off by measles, influenza, whooping cough, diphtheria, typhus, bubonic plague, cholera, scarlet fever and syphilis.

Spreading disease was always intentional on the behalf of the European colonists. Also were many instances that confirm white Europeans many attempts to exterminate the Indians to enslave, and steal their natural resources, land and gold.

"You will do well to try to inoculate the Indians [with smallpox] by means of blankets, as well as to try every other method, that can serve to extirpate this execrable race"
- *Sir Jeffery Amherst, commander- in- chief of British forces in North America, wrote to Colonel Henry Bouquet at Fort Pitt.*

"A war of extermination will continue to be waged between the two races until the Indian race becomes extinct"
- *California Governor Peter H. Burnett, 1851.*

(References Atrocities Against Native Americans-United to end Genocide)

The treachery of Christopher Columbus

Arawak men and women, naked, tawny, and full of wonder, emerged from their villages onto the islands beaches and swam out to get a closer look at the strange big boat. When Columbus and his sailors came ashore, carrying swords, speaking oddly, the Arawak's ran to greet them, bought them food, water, gifts. Columbus later wrote in his log:

"They...brought us parrots and balls of cotton and spears and many other things. They willingly traded everything they owned.... they were well-built, with good bodies and handsome features... They do not bear arms, they do not know them, for I showed them a sword, they took it by the edge and cut themselves out of ignorance. They have no iron. Their spears are made of cane they would make fine servants.. With fifty men we could subjugate them all and make them do whatever we want"

These Arawaks of the Bahama Islands were much like Indians on the mainland, who were remarkable (European observers were to say again and again) for their hospitality, their belief in sharing. These traits did not stand out in the Europe of the Renaissance, dominated as it was by religious popes, the government of kings, the frenzy of money that marked Western civilization and its first messenger to the Americas, Christopher Columbus.

Columbus wrote:

"As *soon as I arrived in the Indies, on the first Island which I found, I took some of the natives by force in order that they might learn and might give me information of whatever there is in these parts"*

The information Columbus wanted most was: Where is the gold? He had persuaded the king and queen of Spain to finance an expedition to the lands, the wealth, he expected would be on the other side of the Atlantic-the Indies and Asia, gold, and spices. For, like other informed people of his time, he knew the world was round and he could sail west in order to get to the Far East.

Spain was recently unified, one of the new modern nation-states, like France, England, and Portugal. Its population and owned 95 percent of the land. Spain had tied itself to the Catholic Church, expelled all the Black Jews, and Black Moors. Like other states of the modern world, Spain sought gold, which was becoming the new mark of wealth, more useful than the land because it could buy anything.

In return for bringing back gold and spices, they promised Columbus 10percent of the profits, governorship over new found lands, and the fame that would go with the new title; Admiral of the Ocean Sea. He was a merchants clerk from the Italian city of Genoa, part time weaver (the son of a killed weaver), and expert sailor.

Christopher Columbus and European Explorers introduce swine to the Native Indians.

Before Columbus voyaged to any part of the America's there were no pigs living on the land.

- At Queen Isabella's insistence, Christopher Columbus took eight pigs on his voyage to Cuba in 1493. They were tough and could survive the voyage with minimal care. They supplied as an emergency food source if needed, and those that escaped provided meat for hunting on return trips. Before this there weren't any known pigs reported in this land.

- But Hernando de Soto was the true father of the "American Pork Industry". He brought America's first 13 pigs to what is now known as Tampa Bay, Fla, in 1539. As herds grew, European explores used pigs not only for eating but for salt pork, and preserved pork. By the time de Soto died three years later, his original heard of pigs had grown to 700. The pigs that escaped and became wild pigs (the ancestors of the feral pigs today), the pork industry was born.

- Pig production spread rapidly through the new colonies. Cortes introduced hogs to New Mexico in 1600 while Sir Walter Raleigh brought the first sows (female pig) to Jamestown colony in 1607.

[*References; A History of Pigs in America, by Mike Vann*]

Pedro Alonso Nino

One of the Nino Brothers in (above pic) Pedro Alonso, he was called "El Negro"

On Columbus's first voyage, Pedro Alonso Nino was the navigator and pilot of the Santa Maria, Juan Nino (his brother) was a master of La Nina, which was the owner, and Francisco Nino (his brother also) is believed to have been a sailor on La Nina. The Ninos also took part in Columbus's second and third voyages. Between 1499 and 1501 they travelled on their own account.

It's also said and noted that had it not been for these black expert astronomers, and navigators Columbus wouldn't have known how to sail or navigate his way across the seas successfully.

[Ref notes; Alice Bache Gould, Nueva Lista Documentada De Los Tripulantes De Colon En 1492]

(Integration) cont.;

In Book Two of his "History of the Indies", Las casa (who at first urged replacing Indians by black slaves, thinking they were stronger and would survive, but later relented when he saw the effects on blacks) tells us about the treatment of the Indians by the Spainards.It is a unique account and deserves to be quoted at length:

"Thus husbands and wives were together only once every eight or ten months and when they met they were so exhausted and depressed on both sides...they ceased to procreate. As for the newly born, they died early because their mothers, overworked and famished, had no milk to nurse them, and for this reason, while i was in Cuba, more than 7000 children died in three months. Some mothers even drowned their babies from sheer desperation...in this way, husbands died in the mines, wives died at work, and the children died from lack of milk...and in a short time this land which was so great, so powerful and fertile...was depopulated...My eyes have seen these acts so foreign to human nature, and now I tremble as I write."

[Reference; A Peoples History Of The United States by Howard Zinn]

Columbus arrival (above) to what now is the U.S was hardly anything kind. He along with his crew sailors enslaved, massacred, and stole gold from the native Indians in the late 1800's

The Elaine, Arkansas Massacre

12 innocent Black men that were given Stays of Execution in the connection with uprisings to kill whites in Elaine, AK 1919

The Elaine massacre was by far the deadliest racial confrontation in Arkansas history and possibly the bloodiest racial conflict in the history of the United States. While its deepest roots lay in the states commitment to White Supremacy, the events from Elaine stemmed from tense race relations and growing concerns about labor unions. A shooting incident that occurred at a meeting of Progressive Farmers and Household union escalated into mob violence on the part of the white people of Elaine (Phillips County), three miles north of Elaine. The purpose of the meeting, one of several by Black sharecroppers in the surrounding areas.

The conflict began on the night of September 30th 1919, when approximately 100 Black sharecroppers on the plantations of white landowners, attended a meeting of the Progressive Farmers and Household Union of America at a church in Hoop Spur(Phillips County). Leaders of the Hoop Spur union had placed armed black guards around the church to prevent disruption of their meeting and intelligence gathering by white opponents. Though accounts of who fired the first shots are in conflict, a shootout in front of the church on the night of September 30th 1919 between the black armed guards around the church and three individuals whose vehicles were parked in front of the church resulted in the death of W.A Adkins, a white security officer for the Missouri-Pacific Railroad, and the wounding of Charles Pratt. Phillips County white deputy sheriff.

The next morning, the Phillip County sheriff sent out a posse to arrest those they suspected of being involved in the shooting. Although the posse had encountered minimal resistance from the black residence of the area around Elaine, the fear of blacks, who outnumbered whites in this area of Phillips County by a ratio of 10 to 1, led an estimated 500-1000 armed white people mostly from surrounding Arkansas counties, but also across the river in Mississippi to travel to Elain to put down what was characterized by them as an "insurrection". On Oct 1st, Phillips County authorities sent three telegrams to Gov Brough, requesting that U.S troops be sent to Elaine.

Brough responded by gaining permission by the Dept. of War to send more than 500 battled tested troops from Camp Pike, outside of Little Rock, (Pulaski County). After the troops arrived in Elaine the morning of Oct 2nd, the white mobs began to depart and return back to their homes. The military placed several hundred Blacks in stockades until they were to be questioned and vouched for by their white employers.

Other whites entered into Philips County to join the action. They attacked Blacks on site once they entered into the county. Over a three – day period, five white men were killed, with an estimated 100-260 blacks murdered, with some estimates it was more than 800 blacks murdered and killed.

From this point forward, two versions of what occurred at Elaine exists. The white leaders put forward their view that black residents had been about to revolt. E.M Allen, a planner and real estate developer who had become the spokesman for Phillip County white power structure, told *The Helena World* on Oct 7th, "The present trouble with negroes in Phillip County is not a race riot. It is a deliberately planned insurrection of the Negroes against the whites, directed by an organization known as "the Progressive Farmers and Household Union of America", established for the sole purpose of banding negroes together for the killing of white people".

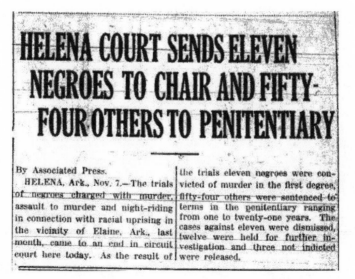

Associated Press, Helena Ark "the Elaine Massacre' of 1919"

(Ref Ferguson, "The Elaine race Riot" master thesis, George Peabody College for Teachers, 1927)

(Ref, The daily Beast)

Elaine, AK Oct 1919

Elaine, Ak, it was reported in some cases there were an estimated 260-800 blacks lynched, killed and murdered by white supremists and towns people during this massacre in Arkansas, Oct 1919.

The Elaine twelve

The Original newspaper article depicting the historic massacre that took place in Elaine, AK Oct 1919

The Reverend Jim Jones Massacre of 1978

California Historical Society / 1974

Cult leader Reverend Jim Jones 80percent of his followers were Blacks

Jones Town,(November 18th 1978), location of the mass-murder and suicide, of members of the California based Peoples Temple cult at the behest of their charismatic but paranoid leader Jim Jones in Jones Town agriculture commune, Guyana. The death toll exceeded 900, including some of 300 that were the age of 17 and under, making this incident one of the largest mass-murders in recent history.

Jones opened his first church in the mid-1950s in Indianapolis. At the time he wasn't affiliated with any particular denomination and had no theological training. His congregation was known for being racially integrated which was particularly progressive at the time (Jones himself was a White European). In 1960 Jones's congregation, by then was called The People's Temple affiliated with The Disciples of Christ, and four years later Jones was ordained in that church.

In the mid-1960s he and his wife incorporated the Peoples Temple in California and settled outside the town of Ukiah with some 100 followers, believing the move would protect them in the event of nuclear holocaust. In 1970 Jones began holding services in San Francisco and by 1972 had opened another temple in Los Angeles. He began to make friends among politicians, and the press in California and had become a respected churchman. Thousands of followers a large percentage of mostly Blacks, had flocked to him. Jones was famous for his" mind reading and faith- healing".

Black members were convinced if they had left The Peoples Church, they would be rounded up by government ran concentration camps, were family members are kept apart. In 1977, after members of the press began to ask questions about Jones's operation, he moved with several hundred of his followers to Jones Town. A compound which he had been building in Guyana for some three to four years.

Jones Town, Guyana

Seventy-Nine percent of Jim Jones followers were Blacks, men, women and innocent black infants.

In 1978, U.S Congressmen Leo Ryan travelled to Guyana to inspect The Peoples Temple's activities and The Jones Town Compound. He was investigating rumors that some members of the cult were being held against their will and that some were even being subjected to physical and physiological abuse. After travelling to Guyana's capitol Georgetown, on November 14th he arrived in Jones Town November 17th, the following day when Ryan was set to return home, several temple members that wanted to leave the compound boarded his delegation truck in order to accompany him back to the United States. Other members attacked Ryan shortly before the vehicle had left the compound. But he escaped unhurt, and the truck continued on with Ryan aboard.

Temple members then launched an attack at the airstrip from which Ryan and his company were to depart. Five people including Ryan, and three members of the press were shot and killed, and eleven others wounded.

Jones Town Massacre

Shown (top), the empty cyanide containers that the Cult Peoples Church members were forced to drink through injections, baby bottles, and cups all orchestrated by cult leader Jim Jones 1978.

1978

It was confirmed that seventy-nine percent of the cult members that was murdered were Black men, women and children, during the Jones Town Massacre.

The Jones Town Massacre 1978

Some of the reported 920-950 bodies that lay dead as a result of cult leader Jim Jones orders 1978

In the wake of the shooting, Jones released radio orders to temple members outside the compound to commit suicide. Shortly thereafter Jones enacted his "revolutionary suicide" plan at the compound, which members had practiced in the past, in which a fruit drink was laced with cyanide, tranquilizers, and sedatives. It was first squirted into the mouths of babies and children via syringe and then imbibed by the adult members. Jones himself died of a gunshot wound. Fewer than 100 members of the temple had survived the massacre in Guyana

Officials had later discovered a cache of firearms, hundreds of passports stacked together, and over $500,000 in U.S currency. Millions more had later been reported to have been deposited overseas.

The Peoples Temple had officially disbanded after the incident and declared bankruptcy at the end of 1978.

It had been reported that there were over 920-950 dead bodies recovered in this mass murder- suicide.

(Reference, mass murder-suicide Guyana, [1978], written by Alison Eldridge)

The Tuskegee Syphilis Experiment 1932-1972

The Tuskegee Syphilis Experiment lasted from 1932-1972, Public Health Service along with the white American government, and the CDC intentionally conducted a fatal experiment on Blacks only.

For forty years between 1932-1972, the U.S Public Health Service (PHS), with the permission of the U.S government conducted an experiment on more than 399 black men in the late stages of syphilis. These men for the most part were selected because they were illiterate share-croppers from one of the poorest counties in Alabama, were never told what disease that they were suffering from or its seriousness. Informed that they were being treated for "bad blood", their white doctors had no intention of curing them of syphilis at all. The data from the experiment was to be collected from autopsies from the men, and they were thus left deliberately to degenerate under the ravages of "tertiary syphilis", which can cause tumors, heart disease, paralysis, blindness, insanity, and death. "As I see it", one of the doctors involved explained, "We have no further interest in these patients until they die".

The true nature of this experiment had to be kept a secret from its black subjects to ensure their cooperation. The sharecroppers were grossly disadvantaged in life which made it easy to manipulate them. Pleased at the proposed free medical care almost all of them had never seen a doctor before, these unsophisticated and trusting black men became the pawns and lab-animals, in what James Jones, author on the great history of the subject, *"Bad Blood"*, identified this as, "the longest nontherapeutic experiment on human beings in medical history"

The study was meant to discover how syphilis affected blacks as opposed to whites. The theory being that whites experienced more neurological complications from syphilis whereas blacks were more susceptible to cardiovascular damage. How this knowledge would have changed clinical treatment of syphilis is uncertain.

When the experiment was brought to the media attention in 1972, news anchor Harry Reasoner described it as an experiment that "used human beings as laboratory animals in a long an inefficient study of how long it takes syphilis to kill someone".

End Results

By the end of the experiment, 28 of the men had died directly as a result of the syphilis, 100 were dead as a result of related complications, 40 of their wives were infected, and 19 of their children had been born with congenital syphilis. At first the men were prescribed the syphilis remedies of the day, bismuth, neoarsphenamine, and mercury, but in such small amounts that only 3 percent showed any improvement. These token doses of medicine were good public relations and didn't interfere with the true aims of the study. Eventually all syphilis medication was replaced with "pink medicine" aspirin. Just to ensure that men would show up for a painful and potentially dangerous spinal tap.

The PHS doctors misled them with a letter full of promotional hype, "Last chance For Special Free Treatment", the fact that autopsies would eventually be required was also concealed .As a doctor explained ;

"If the colored population becomes aware that accepting free hospital care means a post-mortem, every darky will leave Macon County…"

Even the Surgeon General of the United States participated in enticing black men to remain in the experiment. Sending the certificates of appreciation after the 25 years in the study.

One of the most chilling aspects of the experiment was how zealously the PHS kept these men from receiving treatment. When several nationwide campaigns to eradicate venereal disease came to Macon County, the men were prevented from participating. Even when penicillin was discovered in the 1940's, it was known as the first cure for syphilis the men of Macon were deliberately denied the medication. During World War II, 250 of the men registered for the draft and were consequently ordered to get the treatment for syphilis, only to have PHS exempt them. Pleased at their success the PHS representative announced, "So far, we are keeping the known positive patients from getting treatment." The experiment continued despite the Henderson Act (1943), a public health law requiring testing and treatment for venereal disease, and in spite of The World Health Organizations Declaration of Helsinki (1964), which specified that "informed consent" was needed for experiment involving human beings.

The New York Times

Syphilis Victims in U.S. Study Went Untreated for 40 Years

By JEAN HELLER
The Associated Press

WASHINGTON, July 25—For 40 years the United States Public Health Service has conducted a study in which human beings with syphilis, who were induced to serve as guinea pigs, have gone without medical treatment for the disease and a few have died of its late effects, even though an effective therapy was eventually discovered.

The study was conducted to determine from autopsies what the disease does to the human body.

Officials of the health service who initiated the experiment have long since retired. Current officials, who say they have serious doubts about the morality of the study, also say that it is too late to treat the syphilis in any surviving participants.

Doctors in the service say they are now rendering whatever other medical services they can give to the survivors while the study of the disease's effects continues.

Dr. Merlin K. DuVal, Assistant Secretary of Health, Education and Welfare for Health and Scientific Affairs, expressed shock on learning of the study. He said that he was making an immediate investigation.

The experiment, called the Tuskegee Study, began in 1932 with about 600 black men,

New York Times article, by Jean Heller, Syphilis Victims in U.S Study Went Untreated for 40 Years

A group of men who were test subjects in the syphilis experiments.
(Credit: National Archives)

Tuskegee Experiment 1932-1972

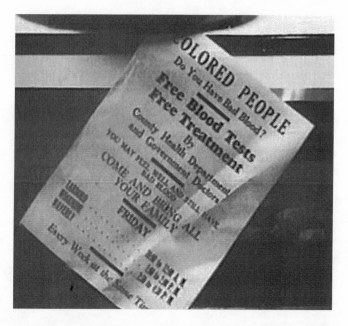

A false Public Health Service advertisement to entice Blacks to get treated for "Bad Blood", Macon, AL

2019 Lexington-Fayette County, Kentucky

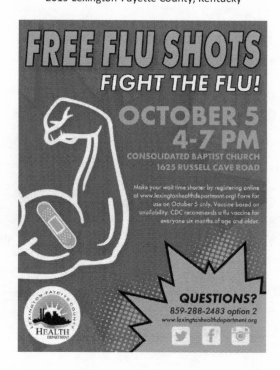

Lexington- Fayette, Kentucky advertisement of Free Flu-Shots 2019, which have proved to be fatal in many cases through-out the U.S

The beginning of the end for the Black Community

Integrate; *to end the separation of people by race,sex,national, origin, etc., in an organization or in society; to integrate is also to combine two or more things to make something more effective;*

The Urban Renewal Act (Project),

Urban renewal (also called urban regeneration in the United Kingdom and urban development in the United States) is a program of land redevelopment in cities, often where there is urban decay. Urban renewal often refers to the clearing out of brightened areas in inner cities to clear out slums and create opportunities for higher class housing, businesses, and more. This process has played an important role in the history and demographics of cities around the world.
Urban renewal is a process where privately owned properties within a designated renewal area are *purchased or taken* by eminent domain by a municipal redevelopment authority, razed and then reconvened to select developers who devote them to other uses.

In some cases, renewal may result in urban sprawl when city infrastructure begins to include freeways and expressways.

In the United States successful urban redevelopment projects tend to revitalize downtown areas, but have not been successful in revitalizing cities as a whole. The process has often resulted in the displacement of low-income city inhabitants where their dwellings were *taken and demolished*.

Eventually became an engine of construction of shopping malls, automobile factories and dealerships, "large box "department stores (like Target, Costco, Walmart, and Best Buy). Thus ,in Washington DC, the famous (or notorious) Southwest Washington renewal project (see Berman v. Parker) displaced thousands of largely Black families, but provided them with no replacement housing because at the time(1954), the law did not provide for any.

[Reference notes, Neil Wates, Urban renewal; US and UK'New Society December 1964, pg. 15]

Redevelopment Project Berman versus Parker

Berman v. Parker was the 1954 U.S. Supreme Court case that approved large scale modern urban renewal, and in the name of "slum clearance" allowed the taking of unblighted properties so the renewal project could proceed on an area-wide basis for the convenience of planners who would not have to bother with establishing slum conditions for each parcel they sought to take by eminent domain.

The Berman project was supposed to reserve at least one third of the new dwellings to be built on its site as low cost housing renting for $17 per room per month. But as soon as the Supreme Court gave this project its imprimatur that provision in the redevelopment law was deleted. The poor blacks that resided there got no benefit from the project. Some 23,000 households were destroyed, and the residents were bulldozed into other, worse parts of the District of Columbia, where they had to pay higher rents for worse dwellings.

[Reference; "Urban Renewal and the story of Berman v. Parker, 42 Urban Lawyer 423(2010)].

District of Columbia 1954, more than 23,000 black residents were removed from their residents by the Urban Renewal Act.

Cabrini Green Urban Renewal Project

Gentrification: the process of repairing & re-building homes and businesses in a deteriorating area, such as urban neighborhoods. Accompanied by an influx of middle-class or affluent people and that often results in the displacement of earlier or poorer residents. (Merriam Webster's dictionary)

Cabrini- Green Homes, which comprised the Frances Cabrini Row-houses and William Green Homes, was a Chicago Housing Authority (CHA) public housing project located on the Near North Side of Chicago, Illinois, United States. They were bordered by the vertex of Clybourn ave and Halsted Street on the north, North Llarrabee Street on the West, Chicago Avenue on the south, and Hudson Street on the east.

Over the years, crime, gang violence and neglect created deplorable living conditions for the residents, and "Cabrini- Green" became synonymous with the problems associated with public housing in the United States. At its peak, Cabrini Green was home to over 15,000 blacks, living in mid-and high –rise apartment buildings totaling 3,607 units. The last of the buildings in Cabrini Green were demolished in March 2011. The near North side formerly home to the William Green projects has been undergoing major redevelopment since the late 1990's, resulting in a combination of expensive upscale high rise buildings and row houses.

1990's before the demolition

Cabrini Green housing Projects constructed 1942-1962, by 1962, ninety-seven percent of the residents that occupied the complex were blacks.

2019 after the demolition

Previously Cabrini Green Housing Projects, now is the result of Urban Renewal, and home to 400k-500k new Parkside Townhomes located in Chicago.

2019, after the Urban Renewal Project

What was once home to more than 15,000 Black residents, now stands very expensive townhomes starting at $499,000.

1990's Before Demolition

Cabrini Green Housing Projects, Chicago Ill.

2019 After Urban Redevelopment

The former area of Cabrini Green Projects, Chicago Ill. Now home to many major retailers such as (above) Target.

White America has in often times shown and historically proven their love and appreciation towards blacks throughout the world, but particularly as it pertains to the U.S. the
odds are always not in the favor of blacks and Latinos more so when it comes to crime,
drugs, gang-violence, single parent homes, lack of income, housing, and a poor educational system.

Once Urban-renewal programs are set in place, the residence that are removed in most
cases have no new address. These are just a few of concepts of reality that most blacks
face in the everyday struggle of urban conditions. Illegal drugs are set in place at a rea-
sonable price, very plentiful, and can be obtained very easily. Soon thereafter addiction
sets in, this leads to desperation, which normally leads to crime then a criminal convic-
tion. This is the vortex of life that America has set in place for most Latinos and blacks in
urban areas. Ultimately for self-destruction.

Toxic illegal Drugs

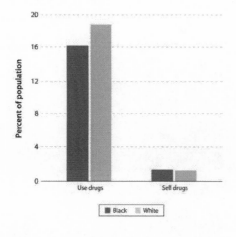

FIGURE 6A.

Rates of Drug Use and Sales, by Race

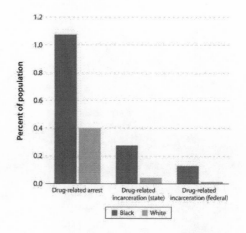

FIGURE 6B.

Rates of Drug-Related Criminal Justice
Measures, by Race

At the state level, blacks are about 6.5 times as likely as whites to be incarcerated for drug-related crimes.

Source: BLS n.d.c; Carson 2015; Census Bureau n.d.; FBI 2015; authors' calculations.

THE HAMILTON PROJECT

BROOKINGS

{Courtesy of The Hamilton Project, Source BLS n.d.c; Carson 2015 Census Bureau FBI
2015}

Blacks and Whites sell and use illegal drugs at similar rates, but Blacks are 2.7 times as likely to be arrested for drug-related offences.

The disparate criminal justice experience of Black in America has played an important role in reform discussions. Differences in incarceration rates are stark: in 2007 a black man between the ages 18and 25 without a high school diploma was more than a white man of the same age and educational level.

Jail (Incarceration)

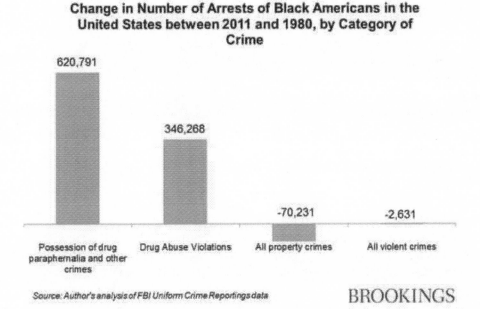

Change in Number of Arrests of Black Americans in the United States between 2011 and 1980, by Category of Crime

620,791

346,268

-70,231

-2,631

Possession of drug paraphernalia and other crimes   Drug Abuse Violations   All property crimes   All violent crimes

Source: Author's analysis of FBI Uniform Crime Reportings data

BROOKINGS

Here's a pretty astonishing chart on the skyrocketing number of arrest of Blacks for non-violent crimes. (Brookings Johnathan Rothwell lays it out);

Arrest data show a striking trend; arrest of blacks have fallen for violent and property crimes, but soared for drug-related crimes. As of 2011, drug crimes comprised of 14percentof all arrests and a miscellaneous category that includes "drug paraphernalia" possession comprised an additional 31 percent of all arrest. Just 6percent and 14percentof arrest were made for violent and property crimes respectively.

Even more surprising what gets left out of the chart: Blacks are far more likely to be arrested for selling or possessing drugs than whites, even though whites use drugs at the same rate, and more likely to sell drugs.

Whites were about 45percent more likely to sell drugs in 1980 according to an analysis of the National Longitudinal Survey of Youth by economist Robert Farlie. This was consistent with a 1989 survey as well of youth in Boston. My own analysis of data from the 2012 National Survey on drug use and health shows 6.6percent of white adolescents and young adults (aged 12-25) sold drugs, compared to just 5.0 percent of Blacks (a 32percent difference).

This partly reflects the racial differences in the drug markets in the Black and White communities.in poor Black neighborhoods drugs seem more likely to be sold outdoors in public in the open. In white neighborhoods by contrast, drug transactions typically happen indoors, often between friends and acquaintances. If your selling drugs outside your much more likely to get caught.

One explanation for drug involvement among black adolescents is the subcultural approach that views drug taking as steaming from the social environment. Residing in inner-city deteriorating poverty stricken neighborhoods is often correlated with involvement in the drug subculture. Many of these young black drug dealers and users live in depressed neighborhoods with intolerable social conditions. They also face racism and discrimination from the White society and often lack economic opportunities. Many often feel a sense of hopelessness and alienation and have low-self-esteem. Drug selling and using provide an escape from these depressing circumstances. Therefore the unfortunate end of this situation is often the dealer and or the user become incarcerated or an addict.

Black men and women become involved with selling illegal drugs because of the temporary financial rewards. In the inner cities, the drug business is one of the biggest employers and pays more in a day in most circumstances than working for a fast food restaurant in a month. After a ten year decline juvenile arrest increased sharply in 1985 especially among non-white youths. The number of arrest for Black youths rose from approximately from 200 per 100,000 in 1985 to twice that amount four years later, whereas that for white youths declined(U.S. Dept. of Justice 1995a).The arrest data for 1994 indicated that 39% of those arrested for drug violation under the age of 18 were Blacks.

Black youths under the age of 18 had an arrest rate for drug violation in 1994 of 483.9 per 100,000 persons, compared with 88.5 per 100,000 for White youths (Federal Bureau of Investigations 1995)

(Ref Journal of Black Studies 2002)

Housing Projects for the Black Community

Farragut Houses, Brooklyn, NY

Public Housing in the United States is administered by Federal, State and local agencies to provide subsidized rental assistance for low-income households. Public housing is priced much below the market value rate, allowing people to live in more convenient locations rather than move away from the city in search of lower rents.

As critics have lamented for years, the Mega public housing projects built during the 1960's and 70's were often so flawed in there design as to harm residents and the neighborhoods around them more than they helped anyone. Most of them were built on super blocks that cut residents off from the surrounding community and that kept police from easily accessing the grounds. They were built in the form of barracks, and imposing towers, neither of which gave residents control over the safety of their communal outdoor spaces.

Brooklyn, NY

Farragut Housing Projects, Brooklyn, N.Y

NYPD

New York City Police Dept.

"There's this combination of all these issues serving to perpetuate that stereotype about people who live there, that public housing itself were bad areas and were a havens for crime," says Meghan Cahill, a researcher at the Urban Institute. " " But in a way they did become havens for crime, it's hard for police to police them, you have a lot of low-income people living there, a lot people who might have been marginalized economically, and not a lot of job opportunities were the housing was built."

(Ref, City Lab, Emily Badger Jan 11th, 2012, Meghan Cahill)

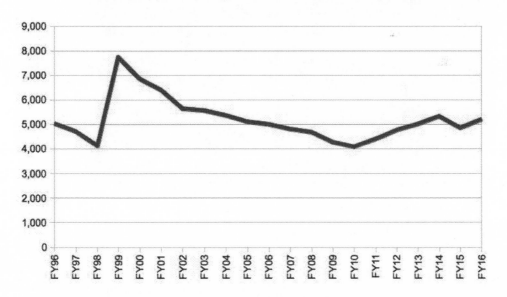

Total Felony Crimes Reported on NYCHA Developments

1996-2016, (*Courtesy of NYCHA*)

With the unmeasurable odds that are not stacked in our favor as Blacks, the U.S government has always intentionally set forth social and economic obstacles for Blacks and Hispanics throughout its history. Indirectly most Blacks aren't aware of the intentional social traps that are placed and packaged before them. Let's use two examples of an everyday occurrence in the Black and Latino communities, and let's break this down with facts, not fiction. Let's start with a business that's so commonly seen and frequently visited by a large percentage of Blacks in their own communities. Liquor stores.

Liquor Stores within the Black Communities,

Liquor Business, Oakland, CA

A University study of 10 cities, including Boston, has found that alcohol especially malt liquor is more widely available in poor, black neighborhoods. The study released, found that poor neighborhoods with a high concentration of Blacks had significantly greater than average number of liquor stores. 40-ounce bottles of malt liquor in coolers, and storefront ads promoting malt liquor.

Malt liquor is of particular concern, the university researchers said, because of its high alcohol volume content and the fact that its 40-ounce containers are sold cold for immediate consumption at a low price. The study also found that the average 40-ounce bottle cost just $1.87, less than a gallon of milk.

"It's cheaper than pot, and cheaper than crack," said Horace Small, executive director of the Union of Minority neighborhoods, which have offices in Roxbury and Jamaica Plain. (Horace Small exec director)

Small said, malt liquor sales are a contributing factor to the myriad of problems that impoverished Black communities face. "Your more prone to have a chip on your shoulder when you have two bottles of that... in you" Small said.

(Ref; The Boston Globe, by Tania deluzurriaga April 3, 2008)

Los Angeles, CA

Researchers at John Hopkins School of Public Health have shown that predominately Black, low-income neighborhoods in Baltimore were eight times more likely to have carry-out liquor stores than white or racially intergraded neighborhoods. Conversely, in higher-income Baltimore neighborhoods a higher percentage of Black residents was not associated with a higher per capita number of off-site liquor stores.

First author Thomas A.Laviest, PhD, MA, associate professor, Health Policy and Management, the John Hopkins School of Public Health, said, "Our data revels an intersection of race and income status that places low-income African American communities at a greater risk of alcohol availability through off-premises liquor stores. Such stores have shown themselves to be an important component of the social infrastructure that destabilizes communities." The study appeared in the June 2000 issue of Social Science & Medicine.

The authors noted that this disproportionate concentration of off-premises liquor outlets is significant and that these stores typically sell alcohol chilled and in larger quantities than in taverns and restaurants (40oz, 64oz bottles), ready for immediate consumption on a street corner, or nearby neighborhood park, or in a motor vehicle that create drinking patterns that more likely to result in excessive drinking, public drunkenness, automobile crashes, and physical violence. Some past studies have further suggested that such drinking behaviors in low-income Black communities also distort Black youths perceptions of what constitutes an appropriate level of alcohol consumption.

(Ref, Johns Hopkins Bloomberg School of Public Health, June 6t 2000)

Lee's Liquor Store at 1656-58 Fillmore Street, San Francisco, CA early 1960's, Photo Courtesy of African American historical and Cultural Society.

Black Single Parenting

Being a single parent is never an easy task, in particular as it pertains to black and Latino men, and women. The odds are always stacked against us on every imaginable aspect of advancement, financial stability, and the mental capacity we endure daily in comparisons to white America. Why are the statistics noticeably higher when it comes to Blacks and Latinos without both parents in the household, why more Blacks and Latinos finds themselves behind bars and incarcerated for failure of paying child support. Was this a well thought out devised plan to add to the destruction and demise of Blacks and Latinos? Are the odds and obstacles set before minorities different life obstacles than white men and women, is there any truth to the term or phrase "White Privilege", does having a black father in the household mean more than we know. Does history provide evidence when the father or a strong righteous black male presence is within the households, morals, integrity, and a great balance of wisdom coupled with the strength of nourishment from black mothers provide more of a threat than white Americans have taught us, why did the United States strategically remove the strong black male figures out of the homes during the Viet-Nam War, just to have heroin produced during this time, and have the black men used as a laboratory animal once again, and to have black men come back to their women full blown morphine and heroin addicts. Ask yourselves once again why does society promote the dis-assemble of black families, meanwhile promote togetherness among the Caucasian families. Is this a coincidence, does society intentionally place life changing obstacles in front of blacks and Hispanics purposely to keep them incarcerated, paying child support, hating one another, leaving the black women alone to support and teach young males how to become men. Why has this vortex of mis-fortune seemingly befall us? The U.S. government was solely placed and founded to control blacks and the minorities, the evidence as we see it in plain view every day is undebatable.

White America has promoted the disassemble of black families, and the feminization of young black males.

By now, these facts shouldn't be hard to grasp. Almost 70percent of black children are born to single mothers. Those mothers are far more likely than married mothers to be poor, even after a post welfare reform decline in child poverty. They are also more than likely pass that poverty on to their children as well. Sophisticates often try to dodge the implications of this bleek reality by shrugging that single motherhood is an escapable fact of modern life effecting everyone from Becky Brown to the "ghetto baby mamas".

Not so; it is a largely low-income and disproportionately black phenomenon. The vast majority of higher income women wait to have children until they are married. The truth is we are now a two-family nation, separate and unequal, one thriving and intact, and the other struggling, broken, and far too often Black or Hispanic.

A disproportionate number of Black children under 18 live in single parent homes, according to new data from the U.S Census Bureau. In its annual "Americas Families and Living Arrangements" data collection, the bureau examined marriage and family, the living arrangements of older adults and other household characteristics.

Broken down by race however, the statistics show stark differences. The percentage of White children under 18 who live with both parents almost doubles that of Black children, according to the data. While 74.3 percent of all White children below the age of 18 live with both parents, only 38.7 of Black children that are minors can say the same.

Instead more than one-third of all Black children in the United States under the age of 18 live with unmarried mothers, compared to 6.5 percent of White children. The figures reflect a general trend: During the 1960-2016 period, the percentage of children only living with their mother nearly tripled from 8 to 23 percent and the percentage of children only living with their fathers increased from 1 to 4 percent. Social scientist have long espoused the benefits of children that live in two-parent homes, including economic, educational, health and other advantages.

(Ref; the Afro-American newspaper,)

(Ref; NEWS ONE April 27th 2011 article)

Fig 1.1 Race, Ethnicity, and Percentage of family groups with only one parent, 2008

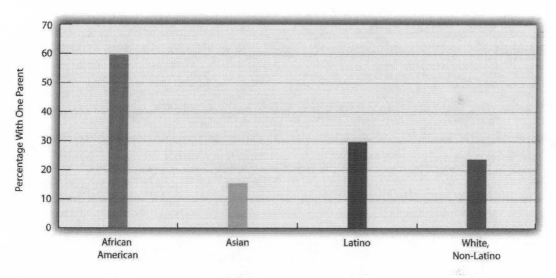

Data from the U.S. Census data Bureau, Washington, D.C. U.S government printing office.

(Ref; U.S Census data Bureau, 2008)

Chapter 3

The Disappearance of Black Culture and Soul

Education

The very understanding of what's your purpose or who you are, you may want to consider having or surrounding yourself with positive, productive righteous learned teachers. For this very reason , after the 14th Century The Italian Renaissance had played a major role in the destruction of Black art which can in most cases relate to Black culture as well. Many have questioned the greatness of Blacks as it pertains to the genius only few can relate to, but many learned scholars can prove. These hidden historical facts were not coincidentally through the years and centuries white-washed, re-done, and very wrongfully taught to our children just because the European and American educational system had nothing at all to do with their time.

This was all intentionally and purposely devised and done not only for White-Supremacy, but also for the purpose to promote self-hate among Blacks and Latinos. As anyone that's a well-studied, well learned, or just an individual that's inquisitive to understand more of the greatness of Black men and women would indeed ask or question, how can a nation of Caucasians that spent most of the early parts of their natural being of existence in the region of Mount Seir 300 years after the flood of Noah. Mount Seir being the land of Edom (Esau), Esau according to historical records is known to be the father and progenitor of the Caucasian race. The question remains how a nation of individuals can come into world power and dominance, whereas the land area and structure that they once inhabited was unbearably cold in climate, living conditions was inhuman among the dark civilized nations which lived during that time in Kings castles, and armored Knight living quarters and also had a unprecedented, supreme set of biblical laws, standards and morals, how as the world knows it today Europeans have made such a deceptive impact on world history as we know it.

During the 14th century during the Italian Renaissance Period which took place between the 1300-1700 is considered one of the most cultural links from the middle ages to modern day history, and to most studied historians and scholars it's also known as one of the most historically deceptive times in worlds history as well.

The Renaissance began in the 14th century in Florence, Italy various theories have been proposed to account for its origins and characteristics, focusing on a variety of factors including the social and civic peculiarities of Florence at the time; its political structure, the patronage of its dominant family The Borgia's, and the migration of Greek scholars and their texts to Italy following the Fall of Constantinople to the Ottoman Turks.

The Renaissance has a long history of debatable arguments among scholars reacting to the very ethnicity of the original dark paintings oppose to the European style-look Caucasian heroes that doesn't at all depict the original art that was re-done, and re-shaped. In this chapter I will share with you, some original paintings that existed prior to the Renaissance Period, that was intentionally white-washed, or tampered with for the sole purpose of hiding the truth of Black greatness.

Original Russian Icon

Russian Icon "Baptism of our Lord" by Andvei Rubliev, 1405. This icon depicts Christ as being a black man and also his disciples that are in the pic are dark-skinned.

Original Russian Icon

Icon Christ entering Jerusalem, surrounded by citizens (Black Jews), of Jerusalem

Icon depicts Christ as having dark skin.

Abraham and Isaac

Above original archive Fresco from Via Latina Catacomb, Rome (cubiculum C) painted about 320A.D. Abraham raises the sword to slay his son Isaac.

Israelites

Dura Europos Fresco worshipping a gold calf. Black Israelites in togas and tunics witness the miracle performed by Elijah with the burning altar that had been soaked with water. Fresco Dura Europos synagogue 244-256CE.

Moses

Dura-Europos synagogue painting: Moses and the
burning bush: 303 B.C. - 256 A.D.

Pictured above, Dura Europus Synagogue, Symbols in the Roman Greco period. Moses pictured
here a dark-skinned Hebrew.

The Good Shepherd

Fresco of The Good Shepherd (Christ) found on the ceiling of the vault of Lucina catacomb of Callixtus in Rome.mid 3rd century. Notice the dark face and legs.

Jonah

The Prophet Jonah being thrown into the sea, Catacomb of Saints Marcellino, Pietro, Cira 300 A.D. Rome. (Notice the dark skin, and in the far top right hand corner a dark hand)

Decorated walls of Dura

All dark images of the biblical prophets surround the Decorated Walls of the Dura Synagogue, 244/45 CE, now in the national museum of Syria, Damascus.

Adam and Eve

2nd-3rd Century painting depicting Adam and Eve from the Catacomb of San Gennaro, (St.Januarius) Napoli, Italy.

Rome

Shown in the above painting Catacombs Saint Pierre at Saint Marcellin, Rome, Christ with ,Magda-
lene tearing a piece off of Christ garment, having negroe facial features, and hair.

Original Black Art

Christ during baptism Catacombs de Saint Calixte, Rome shown with dark skin, and afro-style hair.

Ancient art

Fig.1

Noah praying in the Ark from a Roman catacomb. Shown with dark hands and dark face.(fig.1)

Fig 2.

Inside the interior West Wall of the synagogue at Dura Europos, where you will find all original dark images painted of the ancient Israelites, black prophets and Jews. (fig.2)

Socrates

The great Greek philosopher Socrates shown (above) in this Roman fresco, 1st century BCE in the Ephesus Museum, Selcuk, Turkey. Portrait of Socrates (Athens, ca 469BC-399BC Athens), was a black man living in Athens. Socrates was also known among the citizens of Athens as "The Black Genius"

Socrates

Fig.1

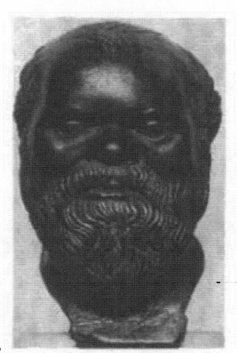

Fig2.

Socrates credited as one of the founders of Western Philosophy, he is an enigmatic figure known
chiefly throughout the accounts of writers and students such as Plato, and Xenophon.

Aristotle

Aristotle, Stone carving Chartres Cathedral, Pertail Royal 12th century shown above, and he too was a black man that lived in Greece.

Aristotle (384-322 BC), was a Black Greek philosopher during the classical period in Ancient Greece, the founder of the Lyceum and Peripatetic School of Philosophy and Aristotelian tradition along with his teacher Plato. He has been called the father of Western Philosophy. His writings cover many subjects, including physics, biology, zoology, metaphysics, logic, ethics, aesthetics, poetry, theatre, music, rhetoric, psychology,poetry,economics,politics, and government. His influence extended from Late Antiquity and the early middle Ages, into the Renaissance.

Aristotle

Aristotle the great Greek Philosopher, Aristotle remained in Athens for nearly twenty years before leaving in 348/47 BC. Aristotle whose name means "the best purpose" born 384 BC. At the age of seventeen or eighteen Aristotle moved Athens to continue his education at Plato's Academy. Aristotle was also appointed as the head of the Royal Academy of Macedon. This (above) is a stone carving that's located in Chartres Cathedral.

William Shakespeare

William Shakespeare 1564-1616, a Black English poet and play wright, considered the greatest writer in the English language and one of the first dramatists. His surviving writings include 38plays, 158 sonnets and 2 long narrative poems. The above picture is one of few original surviving paintings showing his negroe features.

William Shakespeare 1564-1616

English 18th Century original rare portrait of William Shakespeare, in the above photo
you can notice Shakespeare's black features.

William Shakespeare

The above portrait of the great English poet Shakespeare was drawn in the 16th century, and again one of very few surviving original portraits, notice the negroe features that can't be ignored.

Pedro Alonso Nino

Black Navigator Pedro Alonso Nino "El Negro", was a Moor born in Palos de Moguer, Spain. He explored the coasts of Africa in his early years. He piloted one of Christopher Columbus ships in the expedition of 1492, Columbus himself believed the world was flat and had many navigational challenges. Niño also accompanied him and navigated Columbus third voyage that saw the discovery of Trinidad and the mouths of the Orinoco River. Contrary to American history books, Christopher Columbus couldn't navigate his expeditions without Nino's navigational genius.

Ignatius Sancho 1729-1780

Ignatius Sancho (1729–1780) was a composer, actor, and writer. The purported Letters of Ignatius Sancho were edited and published two years after his death.

In keeping with the Albinos nonsense history that says all Blacks in Europe were originally African Slaves, this is the Albinos bio of Ignatius Sancho: He was born on a slave ship in 1729; his precise birthplace is thus unknown. After his mother died in the Spanish colony of New Granada and his father committed suicide rather than live as a slave, Sancho was taken to England and in 1731 was given to three maiden sisters living in Greenwich. While a young man, he met John Montagu, 2nd Duke of Montagu, who took an interest in his education, and in 1749 Sancho ran away and sought refuge with the Montagu families. The Duke had just died but his wife agreed to employ him as butler; when the Duchess of Montagu died in 1751 she left Sancho an annuity of £30 and a year's salary.

Louis Van Beethoven

Louis (Ludwig) Van Beethoven, 1770-1827, was a Black German composer, and pianist. A crucial figure in the transition between the classical and romantic eras in classical music, he remains one of, if the most recognized and influential musicians of this period, and is considered to be the greatest composer of all time. Beethoven was born in Bonn, the capitol of Electorate of Cologne, and part of the Holy Roman Empire. He displayed his musical talents at an early age and was vigorously taught by his father Johann Van Beethoven. At the age 21, he moved to Vienna and studied composition with Joseph Haydn. Beethoven then gained a reputation as a virtuoso pianist, and was soon courted by Prince Litnowsky for compositions, which resulted in Opus 1 in 1795. The piece was a great critical and commercial success and followed by Symphony 1, in 1800. This composition was distinguished for its frequent use of sforzandi, as well as sudden shifts in tonal centers that were uncommon for traditional symphonic from, and the prominent, more use of wind instruments.

(Louis Letronne, Beethoven, 1814, pencil drawing.)

" Frederick Hertz, German anthropologist, used these terms to describe him: "Negroid traits, dark skin, flat, thick nose."

Emil Ludwig, in his book "*Beethoven,*" says: "*His face reveals no trace of the German. He was so dark that people dubbed him Spagnol [dark-skinned].*"

Fanny Giannatasio del Rio, in her book "*An Unrequited Love: An Episode in the Life of Beethoven,*" wrote "*His somewhat flat broad nose and rather wide mouth, his small piercing eyes and swarthy [dark] complexion, pockmarked into the bargain, gave him a strong resemblance to a mulatto.*"

Louis Ludwig Van Beethoven

FIG.1

Black Composer Louis Ludwig Beethoven (1729-1780),above(fig.1)

FIG.2

The death mask of the great Black composer Beethoven shown above (fig.2), with broad negroe nose, and thick lips. Andre de Hevesty says, Price of Esterhazy. During first allegro of Haydn's symphony, asked who is the author, Beethoven was brought forward, "what"? Exclaimed the Prince, the music is by a Black Moor? "Well my fine Black Moor hence forward, thou art in my service".

George Bridgetower

George Bridgetower, a virtuoso violinist that played on stage with Beethoven two centuries ago. George Augustus Polgreen Bridgetower was born in Poland circa 1780, to a Black father and white mother. As a child prodigy on the violin, Bridgetower was taken under wing by England's future King George IV, and received an elite education in music. In his twenties he was introduced to Beethoven. They played in Vienna. Beethoven was so impressed, he dedicated his new Violin Sonata number 9, to "The Mulatto Brischdauer".Beethoven and Bridgetower debuted the sonata together on May 24th 1803. It was a triumph performance.

Unmentioned Original Ancient Black Bust, Coins and Statues

St. Kenelm's Church, Sapperton, Gloucestershire. circa 1100.

English/Saxon Coin
minted in England between the 10th and 11th centuries.

The consideration of evidence of the people that had dark or brunette complexions were indeed among the Anglo-Saxon settlers in England leads on to that people of darker hue, the dark, brown, or black settlers. Probably there must have been some of these among the Anglo-Saxons, for we met with the personal names Blacman, Blacaman, in various documents of the period. The Old English term for darker complexioned Britons brown men or Black men Wealas. (Wealas which is what the new Anglo-Saxon people called the native Celtic inhabitants of England).

Gold coin-pendant, about 590 A.D.
found near St Martin's church, Canterbury.

Cameo of a Black Woman, Gold setting, embellished with Gold and Diamonds - said to be French, 1800s.

Black Royalty in France during the Trans-Atlantic Slave Trade

Cameo of a Black Woman, Gold setting, Richly embellished with Diamonds and Gold - said to be French, but of unknown Provenance

Cameo of a Black Woman, Gold setting, embellished with Ruby's and Diamonds. English - said to be 1800s

Cameo of a Black Woman, made from exotic
organic materials mounted in gold. Made by
Jan Vermeyen (d.1606). He was one of the
favorite artists of Holy Roman Emperor Rudolph
II (1576–1612). The woman may then be his
mistress Catherina Strada: Rudolph never married.

Black Roman Goddess Diana 1650

Cameo of the Roman goddess Diana: made by the Prague goldsmith to the
Holy Roman Emperors, Andreas Osenbruck, circa 1650. Kunsthistorisches
museum Vienna.

Workshop of Girolamo Miseroni 1500s,
Staatliche Münzsammlung. Munich

Negroes In Italy

Bust of a Black man on a Sardonyx
and Gold Ring. Italy, 1500s.

Serpentine Bust of a Black Woman - Italy 1500s

Serpentine Bust of a Black Woman- Italy 1500's

19th century bust of Giovanni Moro, aka, Johannes dictus Morus, Governor of Sicily under Emperor Frederick II. And after 1250, apostolic Camera, and Magister praepositus of Lucera Italy, under Pope Innocent IV

Black King of England, (Black Jews of England)

Edward VI on a Silver Sixpence: There were at least four different coin issues during the brief, six year, reign of Edward VI. His early coins continued to be debased like those of his father Henry VIII, but later the fineness was restored. Our featured coin is a sixpence from the last issue with a facing portrait. The tun mintmark tells us this was struck in London. Chard Gold Britannia Bullion Coins, Lancashire, England.

Black minted coins Barbados 1788

Barbados Penny - 1788

This penny coin was struck in 1788 for use in Barbados and was the first coin to be used on the island. It is thought to have been privately commissioned by Sir Phillip Gibbs, a local plantation owner. The reverse side is a profile of a black man/women with the "I SERVE" text below.

Barbados Penny - 1792

The 1792 coin was minted in England.

King James XII

Great Britain England King James shilling AD 1603-1625

King James I of England, who authorized the translation of the now famous King James Bible, was considered by many to be one of the greatest, if not the greatest, monarchs that England has ever seen. Through his wisdom and determination he united the warring tribes of Scotland into a unified nation, and then joined England and Scotland to form the foundation for what is now known as the British Empire. At a time when only the churches of England possessed the bible in English, King James was to have the common have the bible in their native tongue. Thus in 1603, King James called 54 of history's most learned men together to accomplish this great task.

James who was fluent in Latin, Greek, and French and schooled in Italian and Spanish, even wrote a tract entitled, "Counterblast to Tobacco", which was written to help thwart the use of tobacco in England. King James was a King of Great Britain, France and Ireland. King James was true indeed a Blackman, and the King James Bible is named after King James I of England, who lived from June 19th 1566 to March 27th 1625. The established church was divided during this era. In 1603, King

James called a conference in the Hampton Court in an attempt to resolve issues. As a result, a new translation and complication and approved books of the Bible was commissioned to resolve issues with then translations being used.

King James approved 54 scholars to work on the translation, and 47 worked in six groups at three locations for seven years, comparing to previous English translations (such as The Geneva Bible), and texts in the original languages. The new translation was published in 1611 and called the Authorized Version, because it was authorized to be read in the churches. It later became known as the King James 1611 version.

1.   2.

Portraits shown above 1. And 2, Portraits sketched of King James I of England 1566-1625

(Ref, King James in part, Hebrew Israelite our history)

The Innovative Genius of Blacks

<u>Definition of Invention</u>: *A device, process, or discovery under U.S patent law that is new and useful, that reflects extraordinary creative ability or skill, and that makes a distinct and recognized contribution to and advancement of science. (Merriam-Webster Dictionary)*

Black men and women are without question the driving inventive force behind what we call the United States of America, and to take matters a step further Black men and Women are the creators of this entire universe. Many have wondered and often thought of ingenious ways to contribute to society by the very thought of creating devices, mechanical components, scientific natural medicine, automobiles, farming tools just to name a few. Before the historical but yet brutal Trans-Atlantic Slave trade Blacks were very instrumental in their way of thinking, so far surpassing any European Caucasian understanding, and knowledge.

White Europeans have always as history has it, been very crafty at stealing what doesn't respectfully belong to them, from land to oil and gold. They are creative masters at putting in place treaties, congressional laws, amendments, and constitutions that solely go against the advancement and legal contributions of blacks for generations to come. Classroom teachings will critique and acknowledge only what's given or taught through a higher educational system. But facts speak another. In this section of this book, you will have a full understanding of the creative genius of Blacks, and fully convinced that most of our original inventions were indeed stolen by White America, and their cooperation's.

Lewis Latimer

Lewis Latimer

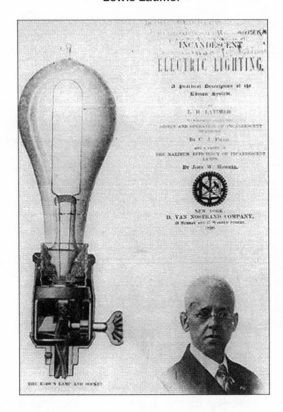

Lewis Latimer (September 4, 1848- December 11, 1928), is considered one of the most important Black inventors ever, for the number of inventions he has produced and patents he secured, but also for the importance of his best- known discovery: a longer lasting filament for the electric light. He also helped Alexander Graham Bell obtain the very first patent for the telephone. Latimer was great in demand for his expertise later in his career as electric light spread across the country.

In 1874 while at the law firm Crosby & Gould which he had been employed, Latimer co-invented an improvement to the bathroom compartment of trains. Two years later, he was sought out as a draftsman by an instructor of children who were hard of hearing; the man wanted drawings for a patent application on a device he had created. The instructor was Alexander Graham Bell, and the device was the telephone.

Working late into the evenings, Latimer labored to complete the patent application. It was submitted on February 14, 1876, just hours before another application was made for a similar device.

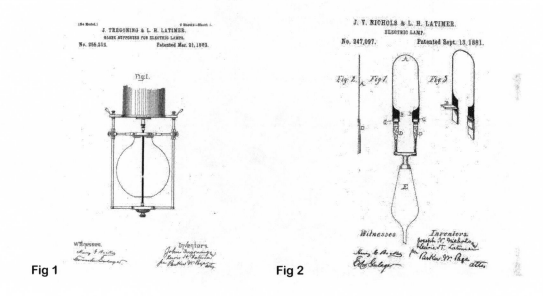

Fig 1

Fig 2

Fig1. Inventor Lewis Latimer developed and invented the electric lamp

_Fig 2. Lewis Latimer invented an electronic lamp with an inexpensive carbon fila-
ment and a threaded wooded socket for light bulbs in 1881, patent number
247,097_

George T Sampson

George T Sampson 1861-1949

Sampson invented what is known today as the clothes dryer, U.S. patent #476,416, was a frame that suspended clothing above a stove so that it dried more quickly. Prior to Sampson's invention, clothes dryers were being invented in England and France in the form of ventilators, which were essentially barrels with holes in them. The barrels would be turned by hand over a fire. Sampson's invention was also a ventilator, but it eliminated the need for an open flame, and used frames instead of a barrel. George T. Sampson is credited for paving the way to more modern clothes dryers. Electrical clothes dryers did not appear until around 1915, and the Hamilton Manufacturing Company produced the first fully automatic dryer in 1938.

Sampson's other known patent for a sled propeller, #312,388, was filed in 1885 and involved attaching a propelling device to a tricycle. The wheels were replaced with runners so it would function on the snow. People occupying the sled would operate the propeller with their feet using pedals. The diagrams for this and Sampson's other patent are still on file with the U.S. patent office today.

George T Sampson

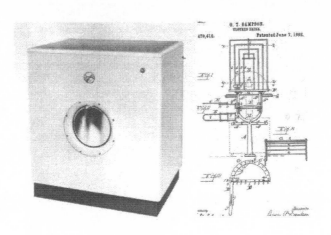

Fig 1.

Fig 2.

Figure 1, the patent for the frame barrel for the electric clothes dryer, Fig 2, modern day dryer.

Robert Flemmings Jr 1839-1919

Robert Flemmings jr July 1839- February 23, 1919, was a Black inventor and union sailor in the American Civil War. He was the first crew member aboard the *USS Housatonic* to spot the H.L. Hunley before it sank the *USS Housatonic*. The sinking of the *USS Housatonic* is renowned as the first sinking of an enemy ship in combat by a submarine. Flemmings finished his naval service on the gunboat USS E. B Hale after June 1865, and subsequently returned to Massachusetts, living and working in Cambridge, Massachusetts, and Boston Massachusetts, where he went into business as a guitar manufacturer and music teacher, and yes Robert Flemmings invented the very first guitar that he called and named the "Euphonica". The U.S Patent Office granted him a patent (no. 338,727.

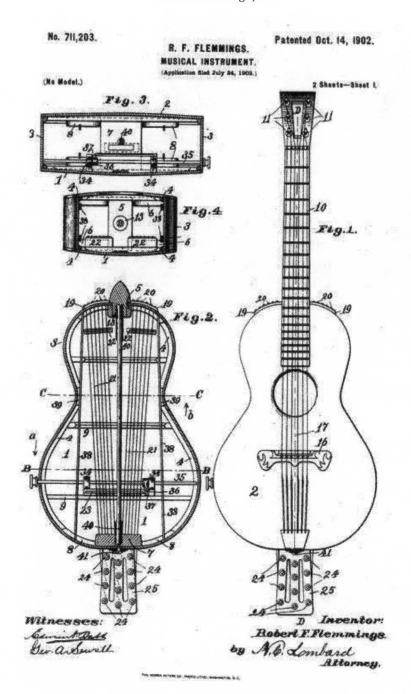

(Ref, Wikipedia, Robert Flemmings Jr.).

John Standard 1868-

   John Standard (born June 15, 1868) was an African-American inventor from Newark, New Jersey who patented improvements both to the refrigerator and the oil stove. Overcoming racial division in the United States at the time, Standard revolutionized the modern kitchen and was granted intellectual property rights to two patents throughout his lifetime.

Standard is commonly attributed with creating the first-ever refrigerator, but the patent issued on June 14, 1891, for his invention (U.S Patent Number 455,891) was a utility patent, which is only issued for an "improvement" on an existing patent. But in all actuality it was the very first ever refrigerator.

Although there is not much known about the early life of John Standard other than that he was born in New Jersey to Mary and Joseph Standard and even less known about his death in 1900, Standard's improvements to kitchen appliances eventually lead to more innovations in both refrigerator and stove designs that would change the way people around the world stored and cooked their food.

John Standards patent invention of the refrigerator

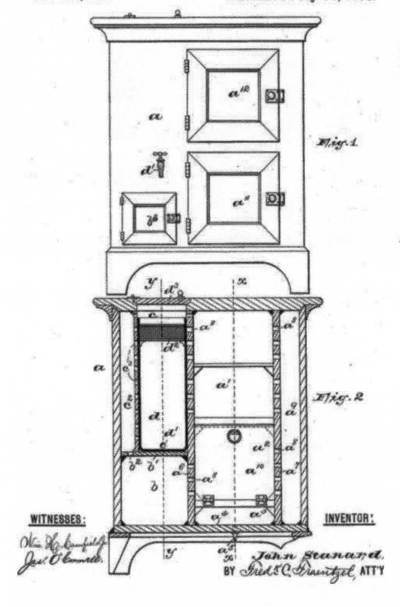

(No Model.)

J. STANARD.
REFRIGERATOR.

2 Sheets—Sheet 1.

No. 455,891.

Patented July 14, 1891.

Fig. 1.

Fig. 2.

WITNESSES:

INVENTOR:

John Stanard.

BY Fred C. Fruntzel, ATTY

Alexander Miles 1838-1918

Alexander Miles of Duluth, Minnesota patented an electric elevator (U.S. pat# 371,207) on October 11, 1887. His innovation in the mechanism to open and close elevator doors greatly improved elevator safety. Miles is notable for being a black inventor and successful business person in 19th Century America.

Elevator Patent for Automatic Closing Doors

The problem with elevators at that time was that the doors of the elevator and the shaft had to be opened and closed manually. This could be done either by those riding in the elevator, or a dedicated elevator operator. People would forget to close the shaft door. As a result, there were accidents with people falling down the elevator shaft. Miles was concerned when he saw a shaft door left open when he was riding an elevator with his daughter.

Miles improved the method of the opening and closing of elevator doors and the shaft door when an elevator was not on that floor. He created an automatic mechanism that closed access to the shaft by the action of the cage moving. His design attached a flexible belt to the elevator cage. When it went over drums positioned at the appropriate spots above and below a floor, it automated opening and closing the doors with levers and rollers.

Miles was granted a patent on this mechanism and it is still influential in elevator design today. He was not the only person to get a patent on automated elevator door systems, as John W. Meaker was granted a patent 13 years earlier.

Miles was born in 1838 in Ohio to Michael Miles and Mary Pompy and is not recorded as having been a slave. He moved to Wisconsin and worked as a barber. He later moved to Minnesota where his draft registration showed he was living in Winona in 1863. He showed his talents for invention by creating and marketing hair care products.

He met Candace Dunlap, a white woman who was a widow with two children. They married and moved to Duluth, Minnesota by 1875, where he lived for more than two decades. They had a daughter, Grace, in 1876.

In Duluth, the couple invested in real estate, and Miles operated the barbershop at the upscale St. Louis Hotel. He was the first black member of the Duluth Chamber of Commerce.

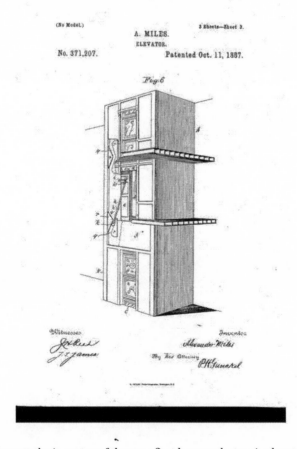

Alexander Miles was the inventor of the very first known electronic elevator, patented Oct, 11, 1887.

Alexander Miles

Alexander Miles not only patented and invented the first elevator, he also improved on his very own invention and patented elevator doors to open and close.

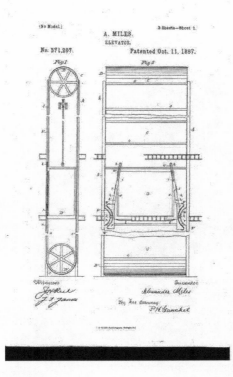

Sara Boone 1832-1904

April 26th 1892, black inventor Sarah Boone received the patent for her ironing board invention. Before her invention, ironing was usually done by placing a wooden board or two on chairs or tables to iron. Sarah however wanted to design something that was more convenient and effective. She also wanted to design something that was easier for women to iron their dresses. She desired something that women could easily iron the body and the sleeves of their dresses on. Her ironing board was made of a narrow wooden board that had collapsible legs and a padded cover. It was also designed to be able to be folded and put away in a closet or other area. Many others had tried to patent a type of ironing board device. However, they were said not to have the sophisticated design of Sarah's. Her ironing board was the precursor for the more modern versions of ironing boards that we have today. She was said to become a household name for those who knew of her invention, and its sleek and sophisticated design.

Sarah Boone was born as Sarah Marshall in the Deep South state of Mississippi in 1832. At the age of fifteen she married a man by the name of James Boone. The couple had eight children together. Soon the family relocated to New Haven, Connecticut. Here, Sarah began her career as a dressmaker. Sarah was also one of the first black women in the United States to receive a patent. She, however was not duly recognized for her work nor for her influence on today's ironing board. Little else is known about Sarah

Boone. Sarah died eight years later after receiving the patent for her invention in 1900. She died in her home in New Haven, Connecticut.

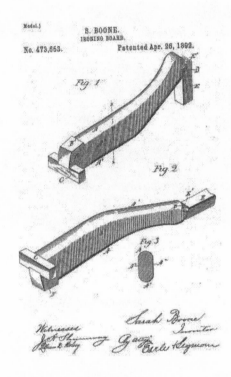

Sara Boone patent and invented the very first ironing board (above), the modern-day ironing board (below)

Joseph H. Smith

Invented the very first rotary head water sprinkler patent #581,785 in 1897

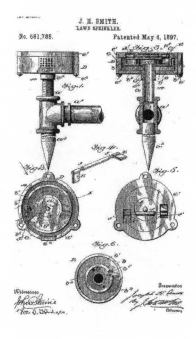

John A. Burr

If you have a manual push mower today, it likely uses design elements from 19th Century black American inventor John Albert Burr's patented rotary blade lawn mower.

On May 9, 1899, John Albert Burr patented an improved rotary blade lawn mower. Burr designed a lawn mower with traction wheels and a rotary blade that was designed to not easily get plugged up from lawn clippings. John Albert Burr also improved the design of lawn mowers by making it possible to mow closer to building and wall edges. You can view U.S. patent 624,749 issued to John Albert Burr.

Life of Inventor John Albert Burr

John Burr was born in Maryland in 1848, at a time when he would have been a teenager during the Civil War. His parents were slaves who were later freed, and he may also have been a slave until age 17. He didn't escape from manual labor, as he worked as a field hand during his teenage years.

But his talent was recognized and wealthy black activists ensured he was able to attend engineering classes at a private university. He put his mechanical skills to work making a living repairing and servicing farm equipment and other machines. He moved to Chicago and also worked as a steelworker. When he filed his patent for the rotary mower in 1898, he was living in Agawam, Massachusetts.

{Reference: Biography of John Albert Burr, ThoughtCo..}

John A. Burr

His rotary lawn mower design helped reduce the irritating clogs of clippings that are the bane of manual mowers. It was also more maneuverable and could be used for closer clipping around objects such as posts and buildings. Looking at his patent diagram, you will see a design that is very familiar for manual rotary mowers today. Powered mowers for home use were still decades away. As lawns become smaller in many newer neighborhoods, many people are returning to manual rotary mowers like Burr's design.

Burr continued to patent improvements to his design. He also designed devices for mulching clippings, sifting, and dispersing them. Today's mulching power mowers may be part of his legacy, returning nutrients to the turf rather than bagging them for compost or disposal. In this way, his inventions helped save labor and were also good for the grass. He held over 30 U.S. patents for lawn care and agricultural inventions.

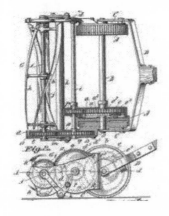

John Lee Love

John Lee Love was an African-American inventor best known for patenting a portable pencil sharpener known as the "Love Sharpener."

Synopsis
John Lee Love was a carpenter in Fall River, Massachusetts, who invented several devices. In 1895, Lee patented a lightweight plasterer's hawk. In 1897, he patented a portable pencil sharpener known as the "Love Sharpener." Lee died in a car and train collision in North Carolina on December 26, 1931.

Background
Little is known about the life of John Lee Love, the inventor of the portable pencil sharpener. It is speculated that he was born some time during the reconstruction period - between 1865-1877. Love later worked as a carpenter in the community of Fall River, Massachusetts. He applied for a patent for a portable pencil sharpener in 1897. His application specified that his invention was an "improved device" that could double as a paperweight or ornament. The design was simple, including a hand crank and a compartment to capture the pencil shavings. It was known colloquially as the "Love Sharpener." The sharpener has been in continuous use since it was first produced.

John Lee Love

Invention of the pencil sharpener 1897

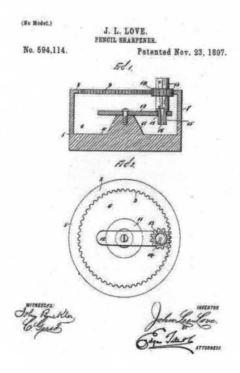

(No Model.)

J. L. LOVE.
PENCIL SHARPENER.

No. 594,114.

Patented Nov. 23, 1897.

William Richardson

William H. Richardson patented an improvement to the baby carriage in the United States on June, 18, 1889. You can view U.S. patent # 405,600 below.

W.H. Richardson improved the first baby carriage. He made the buggy more manageable. He invented the first reversible baby carriage. The buggy designed with a joint in the center that allowed for the bassinet to face towards the person pushing. He invented it so that the bassinet could face the opposite way as well. He also fixed the axels on the wheels so that it is more mobile. His new invention with the wheels allowed it to move into smaller spaces with less trouble.

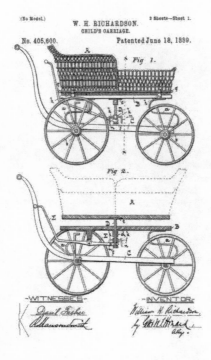

Joseph N. Jackson

       Joseph N. Jackson (1929 –) holds 6 U.S. patents for telecommunications and fertility prediction inventions. Jackson's first patent was for his contribution to a v-chip device that allowed users to block selected content on cable television. This type of technology is commonly used for parental controls. He also holds patents for TV remote control devices. Jackson was not the first person to invent the remote control. The first TV remote controls introduced in the U.S. were created by Zenith in 1950. The remote was called, "Lazy Bones". However it was not wireless. It was attached to the TV by a long cord. Consumers didn't like it because it was a frequent trip hazard. Development of a remote control patent goes back much further-than 1950. The first wireless remote control device, the "Flash-Matic" was developed in 1955 by Zenith engineer, Eugene Polley.

Joseph N. Jackson

The first television remote was invented by Joseph N. Jackson 1978

Another one of Jackson's patents was for a biorhythmic cycle indicator which was a personal fertility predictor. Jackson also holds several patents in the area of air traffic security and tracking systems. Jackson was born in Harvey (Jefferson Parish), Louisiana. His parents were Ernest and Octavia Jackson. At the age of 17, he began working as a maintenance helper at an oil field. At 18, he joined the United States Army where he worked as a ship loader and a military police officer. Jackson received his GED in 1961. He attended television repair school at night and operated a radio repair business part time. He completed a business administration degree at Columbia College in Maryland and also holds a doctorate in Applied Science and Technology, from Glendale University in Santa Fe, New Mexico.

(Reference, rising Africa.org)

Thomas J. Martin

T.J. Martin is credited with improving the design of the fire extinguisher, with a patent issued on March 26, 1872. He invented a system in which water is pumped through pipes in buildings to individual sprinkler heads. The system can be activated by manually turning a valve in the building.

Martin's fire-extinguishing sprinkler system has been in use in the United States since 1874. It was commonly used in large factories as an effective means of putting out large and potentially catastrophic fires. Today, sprinkler systems are required by code in the United States in buildings more than 75 feet tall.

The systems are generally commended for the relatively small amount of water damage they cause to property; they are much more effective than fire hoses at salvaging property. The activation of this kind of system can occur in as little as four seconds. These systems can effectively control a fire before the fire department is able to arrive, resulting in much smaller and more manageable fires. In some systems, heat sensors determine which sprinklers activate, resulting in a much more exact delivery of water and in fewer instances of water damage overall. Systems generally spray water from nozzles mounted in the ceiling of buildings, but some discharge a combination of water and flame-retardant foam.

(Reference, BlackUSA)

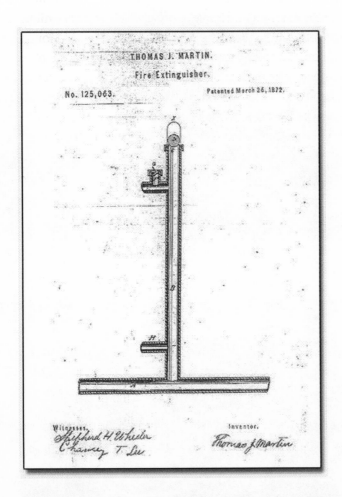

T.J Martins invention of the first Fire Extinguisher 1872

The Beauty of Black Soul and Culture

Black soul and culture is always envied and admired by many, our unique way of flaunting the god-like style so many immolate. Our culture is truly unique from our inner-spirit to our soulfully gifted angelic singing voices. Black Soul is so much more than a fashion statement or a invited trendy-style that's often duplicated, it's a set apart special gift from the Supreme Being that most see but cannot explain, our Black souls are slowly coming back for our great return, but this time, where not going to be ashamed. Step into your greatness and embrace what so many others have witnessed as Kings and Princesses rising-up for that great day of our glory.

(Courtesy of Afro-Sheen)

1960's

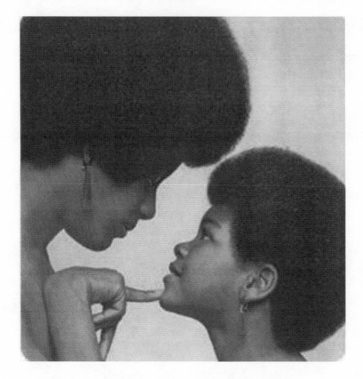

(Courtesy of Afro-Sheen)

Black Soul

Black women are uniquely beautiful.

Black Soul

Martial Artist Jim Kelly

Black Pride

Young Hailee Jones sports an all-natural beautiful hair style.

Just as her daughter (above) Jayke Cunningham mother of Hailee rocks her all- natural curly hair.

Soul R&B Singers

Brothers Jermaine and Michael Jackson

R&B Singer

Chaka Khan

National Basketball Association

Julius Dr.J Erving

Philidephia 76er's Allen Iverson

Musician

Jimmi Hendrix, deemed as the greatest guitar player in history

Award winning R&B legend Diana Ross

Author, historian, writer

Award winning historian, author and writer Frank Zaaqan Jordan 1978

School of learning, contact Zaaqan at <u>zaaqan1212@yahoo.com</u>

For more information, professional historical lectures, book signings please contact Frank Zaaqan Jordan zaaqan1212@yahoo.com

"Never be afraid to learn that which wasn't taught"

More history books written by Frank Zaaqan Jordan

The Holiday Hustle, Controlling the Black Mind and Finances.

This book details how Cooperate America has systematically set in place a debt credit society, which mainly focuses on the Black and Latino community spending and controlling our Black dollars. Black Americans for over 400 hundred years have celebrated and honored Roman established so-called holidays, these days are pagan, and has little to nothing to do with the bible.

Available on Amazon.com

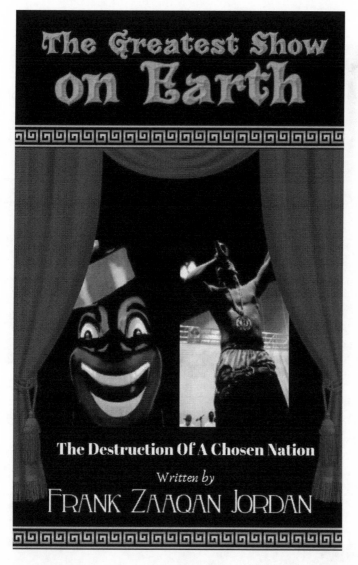

Caucasians have taught and deceived Blacks for centuries how not to love themselves or their own people through what we know today as white supremacy. White Europeans through lies, false history and the media have set a lethal platform for Blacks and Latinos called Christianity, along with self-hate. This book historically details the true history of the greatest people that have ever graced this planet, and their all men and women of color, William Shakespeare, Beethoven, all the prophets and disciples of the ancient world were all Blacks. This award winning, Best-Selling history book will leave you shocked, and enlightened.

Available on Amazon.com

Uncovering The Evil of Amerikka, What The FDA, Pharmacies, And The CDC Fail To Tell You.

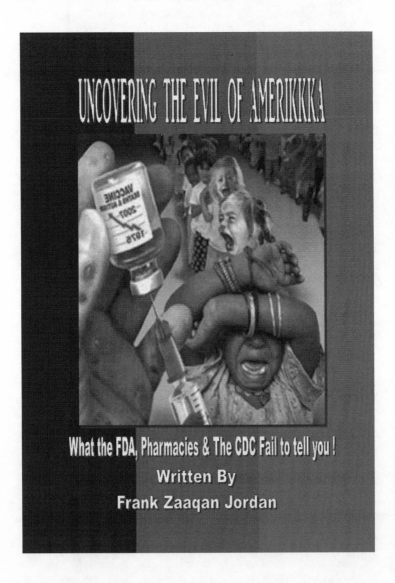

This book has won the 2018 Nat Turner Library Museum Book of The Year Award. The CDC and FDA work hand in hand and continually to approve toxic and in most cases lethal food chemicals into the very food that we consume on a daily basis. Cancer ingredients has been known to be approved by the FDA and CDC to intentionally send patients to get treated, under scientific names these toxic food ingredients go unnoticed in supermarkets we purchase form every day.

Available on Amazon.com

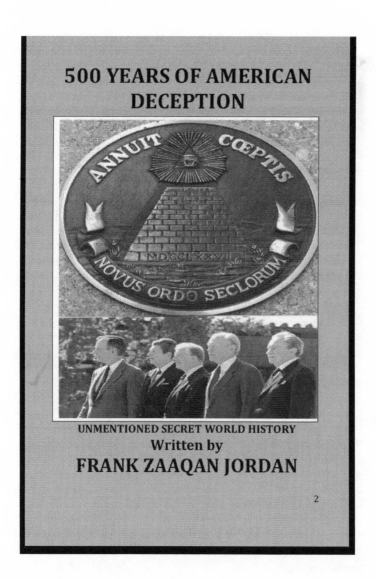

During the 14th Century The Italian Renaissance was one of the most cruel deceptive time periods in the history of man-kind. Famous European painters such as Rembrandt, Leonardo DeVinci along with a host of others were commissioned by the Popes of Rome to attempt to wipe out and "Re-Do" the original Black biblical art, which included the original paintings of all the true biblical prophets, and disciples. This was done over the course of decades, while most people today haven't a clue of why these Popes ordered such an act of man. The truth may shock you.

Available on Amazon.com

Not Just A Coincidence, What Pastors, Leaders, and Politicians Fail To Tell You.

The everyday dilemmas that Blacks have faced in America, from slavery, intentional police brutality, being discriminated against, earning low wages, living in unbearable conditions, generation after generation, one can only surmise or be think to themselves, are these just historical mis-haps or can one say these everyday occurrences are "not just a coincidence" This book takes a historical look at the conditions that Blacks and Latinos are faced and challenged with, historically there is an explanation, this is something your school teacher will not teach you.

Available on Amazn.com

Made in United States
Orlando, FL
15 February 2022